D0474354

Create, Compose, Connect!

Find out how to incorporate digital tools into your English language arts class to improve students' reading, writing, listening, and speaking skills. Authors Jeremy Hyler and Troy Hicks show you that technology is not just about making a lesson engaging; it's about helping students become effective creators and consumers of information in today's fast-paced world. You'll learn how to use mobile technologies to teach narrative, informational, and argument writing as well as visual literacy and multimodal research. Each chapter is filled with exciting lesson plans and tech tool suggestions that you can take back to your own classroom immediately.

What's Inside

- Practical advice on the logistics of using digital tools, such as sending home permission slips.
- A helpful heuristic for analyzing writing tasks by considering mode, media, audience, purpose, and situation.
- Connections to the Common Core State Standards for grades 6 through 8.
- Steps for teaching argument writing by having students consider claims, evidence, and warrants.
- Strategies to help students understand and write digital informational texts.
- Lessons on how to deliver and analyze speeches and other media presentations.
- A section on visual literacy—teaching students to interpret images, signs, and more.
- Ideas for teaching multigenre/multimodal research and suggestions for how students can display knowledge.

Jeremy Hyler is a teacher at Fulton Middle School in Michigan and a teacher consultant for the Chippewa River Writing Project.

Troy Hicks is an associate professor of English at Central Michigan University and director of the Chippewa River Writing Project.

Create, Compose, Connect!

Reading, Writing, and Learning with Digital Tools

Jeremy Hyler and Troy Hicks

Routledge
Taylor & Francis Group

NEW YORK AND LONDON

First published 2014
by Routledge
711 Third Avenue, New York, NY 10017

and by Routledge
2 Park Square, Milton Park, Abingdon, Oxon, OX14 4RN

Routledge is an imprint of the Taylor & Francis Group, an informa business

© 2014 Taylor & Francis

Library of Congress Cataloging-in-Publication Data

Hyler, Jeremy, author.
   Create, compose, connect! : reading, writing, and learning with digital tools / Jeremy Hyler, Troy Hicks.
      pages cm
   Includes bibliographical references and index.
   1. English language—Study and teaching—Computer-assisted instruction.   2. Language arts—Computer-assisted instruction.   3. Computers and literacy.   4. Creative writing—Computer-assisted instruction.   5. Educational technology.   I. Hicks, Troy, author.   II. Title.
   LB1576.7.H95   2014
   428.0071—dc23   2013036807

ISBN: 978-0-415-73470-7 (hbk)
ISBN: 978-0-415-73313-7 (pbk)
ISBN: 978-1-315-81980-8 (ebk)

Typeset in Optima
by Apex CoVantage, LLC

Printed and bound in the United States of America by Publishers Graphics, LLC on sustainably sourced paper.

Contents

Jeremy's Dedication

I want to dedicate this book to the greatest writing mentor that exists, Dr. Troy Hicks; without his help this book would not have been possible. I also want to dedicate this to my family, especially my wife, who has always believed in me and understood why I had to stay awake late many nights.

Troy's Dedication

To Jeremy—and all the teachers we know who share a passion for teaching, learning, and writing: thank you for helping our students create, compose, and connect each and every day.

Meet the Authors

Mr. Jeremy Hyler is a middle school English teacher at Fulton Middle School, which is located in Middleton, Michigan. His primary focus is seventh and eighth grade English, and he works with approximately 120 students on a daily basis. He became a teacher consultant for the Chippewa River Writing Project, a satellite site of the National Writing Project, after attending the Summer Institute in 2010. Since then, he has been implementing new writing strategies along with the use of technology into his classroom. In addition to delivering numerous professional development opportunities to different districts, he has presented at conferences such as the Michigan Reading Conference (MRA), Michigan Council of Teachers of English (MCTE), and the National Council of Teachers of English (NCTE) national conference. In addition to this book, he has contributed chapters to two practitioner books. He resides with his wife and three children in West Michigan.

Dr. Troy Hicks is an associate professor of English at Central Michigan University (CMU) and focuses his work on the teaching of writing, literacy and technology, and teacher education and professional development. A former middle school teacher, he collaborates with K–12 colleagues and explores how they implement newer literacies in their classrooms. Hicks directs CMU's Chippewa River Writing Project, a site of the National Writing Project, and he frequently conducts professional development workshops related to writing and technology. Also, Hicks is author of the Heinemann titles *Crafting Digital Writing* (2013) and *The Digital Writing Workshop* (2009) as well as a co-author of *Because Digital Writing Matters* (Jossey-Bass, 2010); additionally, he has written numerous journal articles and book chapters. In March 2011, Hicks was honored with CMU's Provost's Award for junior faculty who have demonstrated outstanding achievement in research and creative activity. Always learning something new about technology from his wife and children, Hicks resides in Lansing, Michigan.

Preface

As teachers of the English Language Arts, we know that technology continues to affect the interrelated processes of reading and writing, listening and speaking, and viewing and visually representing. We also know that—no matter what new technologies or mandates may come—the power of story, the effective organization of information, and a clear, logical argument are elements that will define who we are as English teachers and how we teach our students.

Words carry meaning, whether printed or pixelated, and we want to help students understand the words of others, as well as create meaning on their own. Thus, we share this year-long look inside Jeremy's teaching through this book, *Create, Compose, Connect! Reading, Writing, and Learning with Digital Tools.*

Jeremy and I share a passion for teaching students how to use digital reading and writing tools so they can become more productive, literate citizens. We met through a summer institute of the Chippewa River Writing Project at Central Michigan University in 2010 and have worked together since then on various professional development activities. More importantly, we meet together in a professional writing group with two other colleagues, and that is where the idea for this book was born. We have worked diligently to create a resource that will help you meet the demands of the Common Core Standards and integrate technology. All the while we have stayed true to our beliefs about how language arts should be taught in a collaborative, experiential manner.

Throughout the rest of the book, you will hear Jeremy's account of teaching and learning with newer technologies in the first person. Rather than have a choppy, haphazard switching of voices from "I," to "we," to the other "I,"

Jeremy and I decided that his voice should take the lead. He has been kind enough to invite me into his thinking; and Jeremy's collegial nature has allowed us to share the process of creating this text. Because of this, we have crafted a book that embodies the best spirit of collaboration: many of the ideas presented have been talked through, written out, and revised by the both of us. We believe the final work is that much more powerful because of our process.

Thank you, Jeremy, for inviting me to co-author this book with you and, more importantly, for thinking critically and creatively about how to employ technologies in smart ways with your middle school students.

—Troy Hicks, August 2013

Create, Compose, Connect!

Two years ago, I was a member of the "cell phone brigade."

I stalked our middle school hallways, keeping watch as students tried to fiddle with devices under their desks. My fellow teachers and I prided ourselves on the fact that we wanted nothing to do with a mobile device or even allowing students to bring their first generation Kindle to class. As a matter of fact, I took pleasure in taking away someone's cell phone. Students began to warn each other not to even think about getting their phones out in class because I had eyes in the back of my head.

But, then something not-so-funny happened. I began to realize that it wasn't necessarily any one device causing the distraction, but perhaps there was another cause. Could it be? Were my students disengaged with my lessons? I do not remember exactly when or how I came to this realization, but it was difficult for me at first because I am still a fairly young, relatively "with it" teacher. No one wants to call himself or herself a "bad" teacher, especially in this era of educational reform and teacher evaluations. Yet, the more I thought about it, the more I realized I needed to start changing my teaching. This wasn't about digital distractions. Even though I took away their phones, my students were still sending me a message. I had to figure out how to connect with them, make my lessons meaningful, and engage them in the types of literacy practices that they were using outside of school.

Before I get any further into this book, you need to know that I am not asking anyone to completely abandon pencils and paper. Nor are we giving up on novels and poetry, replacing them with Web sites and video clips. Most of all, I do not want to suggest that our students can forgo reading and writing in lieu of pursuing only visual or digital literacies, or that teaching with technology—in and of itself—will make anyone a "good" or "engaging" teacher. This is not about appeasing our restless digital natives. In fact, this is the only time I will use that phrase to describe my students because I don't want to set myself apart from them; we are all learning together how to be literate in today's digital world.

Instead, I am suggesting that we invite our students to utilize the mobile devices that they carry with them in critical and creative ways. I say this not simply because I am trying to meet some standard for twenty-first-century literacy, although that is part of what happens. Nor do I say this simply because I feel compelled to meet all the Common Core Standards, although that is part of what happens, too. I say this because the facts are clear, both in my room and nationwide: if adolescents are not engaged at school, then they will find another space to be engaged in, even if that leads to failing courses, dropping out entirely, or worse. So, inviting my students to use their digital devices isn't a novelty; it's a necessity.

For me, integrating mobile technology into my classroom has been a long and very adventurous road, even though it is a path I've only traveled for about two years. My classroom now is quite different from what I experienced as a middle school student, and gaining mutual respect from my students has not come easy. Combating a school policy banning cell phones as well as a computer lab that didn't work created some minor difficulties that could deter most teachers, even me, from wanting to use technology. Yet, after many conversations and e-mails to my principal—as well as support from my broader professional community—my classroom and my school are supporting our students with a mobile lab and the clearance for students and teachers to use mobile devices, such as cell phones and iPads or other tablet computers, in a classroom setting.

I recognize that we are fortunate to have these resources; not all schools have them and, even if they do, they may not use the devices in the best possible ways. So, my experience with using technology is not one where I can tell you how to magically make a one-to-one program appear in your building. Still, I have some ideas to share that have worked for me and other teachers with whom I have collaborated. I want to show you how my students are not only more engaged in my classroom but are better digital citizens because of using technology. I enjoy watching my students write more, work more, collaborate, and consistently stay focused on the task at hand. Rather than banning technology and mobile devices, I have embraced them as significant classroom tools. Distractions do still occur, yes. However, my students these days are more in tune with what's happening in my classroom now that they can use these tools than were my students of just two years ago.

How does this happen? At the core, my students and I have a mutual respect when it comes to mobile devices and technology. I know that they want to use these tools that are in their pockets and backpacks and that the Internet pervades their daily life, especially outside of school. As I have come to understand more and more about what it means to be a reader and writer in the digital age, I have had to learn along with my students. Let me share an example.

At the end of the 2009–2010 school year, I began my journey with mobile devices by experimenting with cell phones in the classroom, but like most first-time efforts at teaching anything, I didn't have much success. With the exception of our library computer lab, which had newer Apple desktop computers, our school's technology was mediocre at best. So, after careful observation of my students, I invited them to bring their cell phones to my class, and I simply had them respond to a writing prompt I put on the board. They responded by sending a standard text message to another classmate within the room. I believed in the idea of "no matter where students are—at the movies, at a ball game, in their bedroom—they love to send and receive text messages" (Kolb, 2008, p. 114). And, indeed they do! From there, I encouraged them to reply to anyone who sent them a message. I did not have any written guidelines for them to follow; they would just send a text and respond to someone who sent them a text, and of course, all messages had to be appropriate for school.

You can probably see where this is going, right? Needless to say, it wasn't a very successful experiment. First, my students were constricted to just talking with students whose cell number they already possessed. Second, I was literally breaking a sweat as I bounced around my classroom trying to read what my students had written in a text and who they sent it to. My head was spinning, despite the fact my students were using technology in the classroom, and they appeared to be more engaged. I had lost focus of why I was using the technology in the first place. Using the phone had to be about intentional reading and writing, not just using technology just for the sake of using technology. I needed to educate myself more on how I was going to use mobile devices, such as cell phones, in my classroom. I didn't realize what I was in for during the summer of 2010.

Before I tell you what happened that summer, I need to share my thinking about professional development (PD). In the 12 years that I have been teaching, I have had the privilege to be a part of many wonderful PD opportunities. Like most teachers, I have participated in PD that has been off-the-charts excellent. I have also attended sessions where I wish I hadn't spent two hours putting together lesson plans for a substitute teacher; the PD where the best thing is the turkey sandwich at lunch time. The purpose of PD is to give us lessons, units, and tools to take back to our classroom for future implementation. Teachers especially want to feel reenergized and excited, ready to go back into the trenches the next day with new tools in hand. Better yet, we want to have more than lessons or tools. We want to feel like we have a new focus, a new energy and purpose for working with our students. All that—and a bag of chips—would be nice, but it doesn't happen all that often.

So, I wasn't quite sure what I was in for when, during that summer of 2010, I set aside four weeks to attend the Chippewa River Writing Project Summer Institute at Central Michigan University. Little did I know, it would be the best PD I would ever participate in. It completely changed how I looked at writing instruction in my classroom, and it also opened the door to learning many digital tools that I quickly looked to implement into my classroom. This is where I first met Troy, as well as a number of other wonderful colleagues from mid-Michigan. We spent time working on our own writing, responding to writing by others, and participating in teaching demonstrations. What excited me even more than all that was the fact that we created purposeful digital writing: wikis, Google Docs, digital stories, and more.

In addition, I gained firsthand experience, which proved to be beneficial, with the Common Core State Standards (CCSS), the full implementation of which was, at the time, looming for the year 2014. When we would plan our own teaching demonstrations, we would outline our intentions and what we believed about teaching writing, and our colleagues would then write us collaborative responses in the form of letters. In those letters, one element that we discussed was how the presenting teacher made connections to state and national standards. Thus, I was given the opportunity to collaborate and bridge standards from the current state curriculum to the CCSS, and that began what has now become a three-year conversation about the CCSS, especially the three major text types: narrative, informational, and argument.

Since then, I feel that energy and excitement every single day I step into my classroom, and I have also wanted to learn more about using mobile devices. Of course, I am still learning. Even as Troy and I collaborated on this book during the 2012–2013 school year, I kept trying new ideas and revising old ones. Our writing group gave us feedback on the drafts, and that fueled our passion to keep writing and integrating technology in thoughtful ways. I'd come a long way since I'd stalked the halls for cell phones. And, I've still got a long way to go. This book has been an opportunity to capture my thinking and remind me that I am still on the journey.

Finally, before we get into the substance of the book—the technologies and strategies used in my language arts classroom throughout the entire school year—we want to share a little more of our thinking about mobile devices and other technologies that relate to teaching in the twenty-first century.

Using Mobile Devices and Web-Based Tools to Teach Language Arts

Mobile devices such as laptops, cell phones, tablets, and e-readers allow individuals to access data and information from wherever they are located. It is estimated that by the year 2016, every student is going to be using mobile learning to some capacity. The 2012 K–12 Horizon Report states that mobile adoption is less than one year away in most schools across the United States, and by the time this book is published, we will know if that prediction has come true (New Media Consortium, Consortium for School Networking, & International Society for Technology in Education, 2012). The Pew Internet and American Life Project reports that over 70% of teens have their own mobile device and that over 90% are using the Internet on a regular basis (Lenhart, Arafeh, Smith, & Macgill, 2008). We have to remember that, even though almost all of the students are using these devices for social networking, many are using them for academic purposes as well as blogging, gaming, programming, and other entrepreneurial enterprises. In short, students are using mobile devices. So, why aren't we inviting them to use these devices in our classrooms?

There are many answers, of course, but it boils down to this: using mobile devices in the classroom changes the dynamics of how we educate our children today. Done well, this change in learning can be an incredibly powerful one. Mobile devices have powerful processors, built-in HD video cameras, faster networks, cloud storage, and they are cheaper than computers. Students who swarm our classroom every day have been surrounded by technology their whole lives, and if we teachers can find a way to integrate mobile devices into our classrooms, our lessons will become more attractive to our students.

Embracing the use of personal devices in a classroom setting is becoming more attractive than ever before. School districts are beginning to implement use of iPads and other tablets into their classrooms. This year at my wife's school, every child from grade 6 through 12 has received an iPad, and so have the teachers. An interview in 2010 with Mark Warschauer, a professor in the department of education at the University of California, Irvine, who is acknowledged as one of the leading academics studying technology's effect on education, is quoted in an article by Kahney as saying, "You can do a lot of the stuff you can do on laptops, but [iPads] are great for reading, especially as textbooks go into the digital realm" (Kahney, 2010). Warschauer's forward thinking has led school districts to a better understanding of how these types of devices can be beneficial. He outlined a number of keys to success in his book *Learning in the Cloud: How (and Why) to Transform Schools with Digital Media* (2011), noting especially that technology in and of itself does not create educational reform. Instead, it is only a combination of factors—including a strong vision, specific plan, strong infrastructure, supportive professional development, and thoughtful evaluation—that has the potential to transform schools.

While teachers and school districts look for new ways to engage today's learners, the use of technology, specifically mobile devices, can bring promising changes to a classroom where reading and writing are at the center each and every day. When we as educators consider visual literacies and the role of social media and other digital literacies, such as blogs or wikis, then the shift to the digital age cannot be ignored. Therefore, students need to be more engaged with these twenty-first-century literacies that can be accessed through mobile devices. Leading experts in cell phone use Lisa Nielsen and Willyn Webb state in their book, *Teaching Generation Text*, "Showing how cell phones can be used to enrich instruction, engage learners using research-based instructional strategies, and enhance the classroom practices you already are using can convince administration, parents, and guardians that incorporating cell phones into instruction makes sense" (2011, pp. 67–68). Troy and I both argue that, more than simply making sense, teaching with digital devices is a pedagogical imperative; English teachers have always fought for students' literacy, and this is the next frontier for our advocacy.

On the other hand, educators in an English classroom are reluctant to make the necessary changes to accommodate our students who are constantly engaged with their handheld devices. The reluctance of these educators comes from a lack of knowledge about mobile devices and a lack of familiarity with the apps being used (remember, I have been here, too, once being a proud member of the "cell phone brigade"). Some teachers feel that these devices are more of a distraction and that the use of them will make it so that the students won't stay focused. There is a general fear that allowing the use of mobile devices is opening a Pandora's box, and there will constantly be issues with students using them within the classroom when they should be paying attention to instruction. Moreover, teachers feel they don't have time to learn something new, especially with the implementation of the Common Core State Standards

(CCSS). Kelly Gallagher even states in his latest book, *Write like This: Teaching Real-World Writing through Modeling & Mentor Texts*, "Technological devices, so pervasive in today's culture, work against fostering thoughtfulness; instead, they crowd thoughtfulness out of our student's lives. They create smart children who are ignorant about the real world" (2011, p. 61).

Gallagher is wise enough that he doesn't blame the technology alone, nor does he feel that we should completely abandon it. If students aren't being thoughtful due to technology, then it is our job as educators to show them how to be thoughtful and innovative. As I said before, we need to take a hard look at our teaching. Don't get me wrong; I don't feel the responsibility falls just on our shoulders, but if we are in the midst of a paradigm shift in how we teach our students, then digital citizenship should be addressed with our students and their parents. Jason Ohler reminds us that "digital venues can bring out the best or worst in its citizens" (2010, p. 51). If students can learn in a safe, secure environment, it can propel them to take that attitude outside of the classroom. Finding effective strategies to implement in the classroom doesn't have to be challenging and time consuming. Again, that is our hope for this text; for teachers to locate quick, innovative ways to help the students develop constructive uses of their mobile devices.

Closely related to this is the idea that students must create, not just consume, digital media. Just because we have invited students to use mobile devices in our classrooms does not mean that they will suddenly be more engaged or become smarter simply for having used them. As the teacher, as well as the adult in the room, I need to make sure that I am modeling the types of literate skills and productive behavior I want my students to use themselves. Just because a student sends a text, posts a status update, or creates a short digital video doesn't mean that he or she has considered audience and purpose, as well as how best to meet the requirements of a writing task.

Also, and he probably wouldn't say this himself, Troy knows a thing or two about teaching with technology and I will use some of his words to segue into this discussion about how we can keep the focus on our students and their needs, no matter what devices they are holding in their hands:

> As we consider the students with whom we work each day, we can easily fall into a pattern of stereotyping that positions them in different, sometimes unflattering ways. For instance, we may see them as digital natives, yet they may not have the skills and abilities to create and critique all kinds of digital media that they consume. We may also see them in the trappings of adolescence, acting in

their own self-interest and without regard for consequences . . . [however, in order to help them succeed] we need to rely on the technical expertise and interpersonal skills that they have and guide them in ways that will help them learn about digital writing. (Hicks, 2009, p. 129)

We know from years of educational research, as well as our own professional experiences, the teacher standing in front of the classroom is the most significant factor in regards to student achievement. "This means that student achievement can be enhanced by teachers who focus on helping their students develop strategies for reading and writing within their respective content areas" (National Council of Teachers of English, 2011). We need to think about how our perceptions and use of mobile devices and digital media—and, by extension, our perceptions of our students who use them—can make a difference in the lives of our students.

One other strategy that I learned in that 2010 institute from the Chippewa River Writing Project was that analyzing the writing task could become a central part of my teaching. Troy introduced us to a thinking tool, a heuristic that he learned from his teaching mentors: MAPS. In *The Digital Writing Workshop* (2009), Troy describes the rationale behind MAPS in the following manner:

A digital writer constantly questions the ways in which a text is being produced—from the purpose and audience to whom she is writing, to the choice of technologies used to compose a text, to how that text is distributed—and MAPS helps writers make those decisions. (p. 56)

The MAPS heuristic includes the following components:

- mode—the genre of a particular piece of digital writing;
- media—the form in which the digital writing is produced including text, image, audio, video, or Web-based;
- audience—the intended audience (usually a teacher) and incidental audiences (such as peers, parents, or the broader online community);
- purpose—the broad academic purpose (e.g., to inform, to persuade) and the writer's own purposes (to describe and define a topic of his or her choosing in detail);

- situation—the factors affecting the writer himself or herself (e.g., personal writing skills and habits), as well as the context for the writing (e.g., deadlines and options for production).

As we continue to explore how to integrate mobile devices and Web-based tools into language arts instruction, we will take time in each chapter to refer to the MAPS heuristic, offering you some guiding statements that can help frame your instruction and assessment. In short, MAPS can be used as a tool for you to teach digital reading and writing, and we aim to show you how.

A Year in My Classroom

Since I have begun welcoming students to use their devices in my classroom, the changes have been incredibly positive. I have developed some beliefs that I felt, and still feel, are extremely important. First, students have been and continue to be genuinely excited about writing. Second, I have opened the door for students to see that mobile devices can be used for much more than watching YouTube videos and accessing Facebook. They see their devices as a means to accomplishing important tasks. For example, at the time I first introduced mobile devices, my eighth graders were working on a multigenre research project; I had two eighth graders using their cell phones. They had downloaded the Google Drive application on their phone and were typing a piece that was part of their project. Third, reading, writing, collaborating, and self-directed learning are taking place in my classroom, and they are taking place at an intense rate because students feel ownership while using mobile devices. Overall, while teaching middle school language arts has its ups and downs, and I do still have the occasional discipline problem, mobile devices generally enhance my students' learning.

So, what does all this mean for them, as readers and writers, listeners and speakers, viewers and visual representers? What does it mean for me as a teacher? I now welcome you to think with me through the process of setting up my classroom—from the first weeks of school through a number of unit plans—to see how I invite students to create, compose, and connect to the language arts, devices in hand.

Throughout the rest of this book, Troy and I hope you not only get the metaphorical "turkey sandwich" that I mentioned above but that you can take away many reasons to use mobile devices in the classroom and a newfound energy to take back to your students. Here is a brief outline of where we will go, based on how I have structured the units for my seventh and eighth grade classes. You may choose to skip around a bit and look at the chapters that are most relevant for your own teaching at this moment or based on what you plan to teach for your next unit. As a matter of fact, I encourage you to jump around. There are always certain areas I need more help with when it comes to my classroom. I may buy a book that is all about language arts or technology, but I may spend more time placing sticky notes under the argumentative section of the book because this is an area where I need improvement on as a teacher. In each chapter, Troy and I have worked to thoughtfully connect the instructional approach with an appropriate technology, so there are many examples of lessons and, where appropriate, student work as well.

Chapter 2: Building a Classroom (and Virtual) Community

Building a community where students feel comfortable to write and share their writing sets the stage to have a more successful year. Google Docs introduces the students to the world of collaboration and helps them be more successful with peer editing and revision. A tool such as Schoology allows students to access assignments, rubrics, and articles of the week throughout the year. Cel.ly is a superb tool for cell phone users and can be used for literature circles. Grammar Girl and Dictionary.com are tools accessible on any platform for students to use all year. Setting up a classroom where mobile devices are used can be rather tricky and time consuming. From permission slips to everyday apps, setting the stage for all these tools paves the way for smoother teaching and learning.

Chapter 3: The Rest of the Story: Reading and Writing Narratives

Everyone has a story to tell! The first big unit I begin the year with is my narrative unit, where I use word clouds, digital stories, and voice recordings to enhance the learning experience. From beliefs to memoirs to poetry, students engage with numerous apps and mobile tools to craft their stories with narratives. From word clouds using Wordle.net to the use of Google Drive and utilizing resources such as National Public Radio's "This I Believe," chapter 3 is only the beginning for my students' immersion into technology and the Common Core State Standards.

Chapter 4: Reading Our World, Writing Our Future (Informational)

Understanding informational text is vital and being able to create it is even more so. Intended audience, author's purpose, and reader's opinion can be brought to light with tools such ScreenChomp, Evernote, and Twitter, as well as blogs and wikis. Students will learn how to determine what is important to post on Twitter because they only have 140 characters to work with. In addition, middle school students explore book reviews and myths.

Chapter 5: Looking for Evidence (Argumentative)

It is hard to believe you have to teach a middle school student how to argue effectively! But, there is more to an effective argument than just shouting loud enough. This chapter will take a look at the steps I take with my students to teach effective argumentative strategies while using Capzles, Prezis, and Venn diagram apps. Students become more engaged in this challenging genre of writing using George Hillocks's book *Teaching Argument Writing, Grades 6–12: Supporting Claims with Relevant Evidence and Clear Reasoning*, focusing on claims, evidence, and warrants (2011).

Chapter 6: Can You Hear Me Now? (Speaking and Listening)

Speaking and listening skills are just as important with the CCSS. Students need to be able speak clearly in a collaborative setting or when giving a speech. In addition, students should be able analyze the purpose of any diverse media presentation where listening skills are involved and evaluate what is behind the motives of the presentation. Tools such as Prezi can be used for these standards.

Chapter 7: Seeing Isn't Always Believing (Visual Literacy)

Visual literacy is gaining momentum every year in all classrooms, even higher education, as well as the job market. Students learn to interpret, negotiate, and take meaning away from images, signs, and other visual representations in my classroom. I introduce screen-capturing tools such as Snagit and also incorporate Skitch into the visual literacy lessons presented to students.

Chapter 8: Our Many Voices (Multigenre Research Project)

The CCSS suggests students participate in a research project. Using ideas from Tom Romano's multigenre approach (Romano, 2000), my students explore different genres of writing while focusing on just one topic of their choice through a variety of different media. Students also have choices in how they display the knowledge they have learned, using Glogster, Toondoo, and other tools on their mobile device to enhance their projects.

Afterword

Here, Jeremy takes a few pages to wrap up his thinking on the entire school year, as well as reflecting on the process of writing the book.

Our goal in sharing these lesson plans and technology strategies is not that you will use every single one of them immediately in your classroom. I have been fortunate enough to have opportunities to integrate it all, but your path may be slightly different. And, that's OK. We have them all listed for you here on our book's companion Web site (createcomposeconnect.wikispaces. com), and for those of you reading this as an e-book, you can click on the links directly and check out the tools.

Troy and I hope you are able to find strategies that work for you. We want you to advocate for your students and their ability to use these devices for authentic, academic purposes and invite them to create, compose, and connect across all the language arts throughout the year.

Building a Classroom (and Virtual) Community

The dynamics of my district are such that only seventh and eighth grade students are at the middle school. Seventh graders are already overwhelmed finding their way around a new building with new classes, remembering locker combinations, and just falling into a routine. So, when they come into my classroom and I ask them to take out their cell phones, it can be even more confusing for them!

I am not teaching in a school where I have every new piece of technology at my fingertips. I teach in a small, rural school district where my seventh and eighth grade combined makes up 120 students, approximately 60 students in each grade, totaling four classes a day. Teaching in such a school and community can be both challenging and rewarding. Not every student I work with on a daily basis knows how to use technology to its fullest potential. I have students who don't have access to the Internet at home, and I have students who do not possess any type of mobile device. It is safe to say less than 60% of my students have online access with a computer outside of school, even though Wi-Fi is becoming more and more popular in public spaces, as are businesses where they could access the Internet (Troianovski, 2013). On the other hand, my students do know of the mobile devices available to them. To help me learn about the digital tools they know and use, I conduct a quick poll at the beginning of the school year that yields a number of responses (Table 2.1).

Not only can it be concluded that my own students are aware of the different mobile devices, but research shows that "teens have access to other mobile devices that connect them to other people and other networks. The most prevalent of these devices are mobile gaming devices like the Nintendo DS and DSi and the Sony PlayStation Portable (PSP)" (Lenhart 2009, 12). There

Table 2.1 Technologies That Students Use

1. Laptops	6. iPad
2. Cell phones	7. iPod
3. Kindles	8. iPod Touch
4. PSP	9. Nexus
5. Nintendo DS	10. Tablets

are a number of my students who do own these same devices. The number of students who own these devices in my classroom is comparable to national statistics. "Mobile gaming devices are owned predominantly by younger teens (those ages 12–14). Two-thirds (67%) of 12–14 year olds own a portable gaming device, compared with 44% of teens ages 15 to 17" (Lenhart 2009, 12). Whether we are looking at gaming devices, e-readers, smartphones, or laptops, students are aware of the tools available to them.

By looking at the tools my students have available to them and the tools I have available to me, it is only then I can make the decision of what to incorporate into my classroom. Thinking about implementation can be perplexing. It is important to remember not to get overwhelmed with choosing what to use in the classroom. Simplicity can be the most effective. For example, a teacher could incorporate two different tools into his or her classroom per year and essentially master those specific tools in a year. If the teacher did this for the next five years, he or she would have a total of 10 tools for use in the classroom. And with the CCSS already asking us to integrate technology into our lessons, this book offers some practical strategies for delivering that digital content in the language arts classroom. I don't feel teachers need to completely reinvent the wheel when it comes to creating new lessons and units, especially when integrating technology. As a matter of fact, it is always smart to have plan B in place, usually involving paper and pencils. A teacher never knows if there are going to be problems with Web sites, applications, or the equipment itself. Believe me, I have experienced all three. And, quite honestly, sometimes it is best that students unplug from technology to do their reading and writing. Still, my overall approach involves explicit instruction in the genre we are exploring as well as the technologies being used.

Mobile devices should enhance your daily CCSS lessons and overall units. For myself, professionally, I needed to make an overhaul to my lessons and units. Our board of education adopted the CCSS starting the 2011–2012 school year. After one year of implementation, I have a more solid grasp of how I am meeting the standards in my classroom. Throughout the book, as I mention the CCSS I will be referring to my seventh grade version of the Common Core

Flipbook (Bainbridge & Holman, 2011). In addition, MasteryConnect has a mobile app that is easy to read and is very convenient. As you can see in Images 2.1 and 2.2, it is a quick, handy resource that includes the standards and College-Career Readiness statements for students.

When a teacher considers the question, What is the purpose of students using mobile devices in an English class?, we need to step back and realize that students are indeed still reading and writing. Also, students can embrace

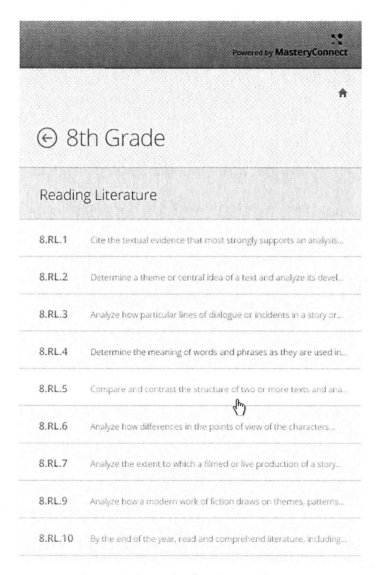

Image 2.1 Screenshot from MasteryConnect

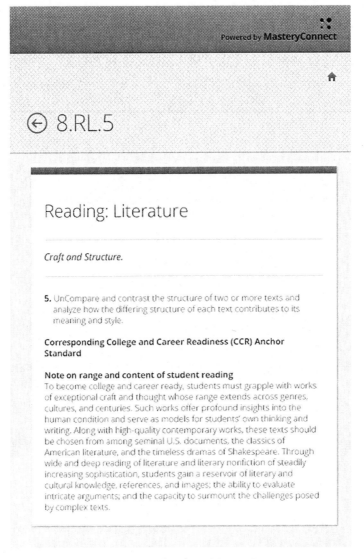

Image 2.2 Screenshot from MasteryConnect

the other aspects of language arts (listening, speaking, etc.). As I experiment and use mobile devices in the classroom more and more, I am starting to appreciate the simple fact that my students are indeed *writing*, whether it is their text language on their cell phones or more formal in a response they have composed on a social media site. Often, they don't see these activities as writing (MSU News, 2010). Students need to realize that they have learned valuable writing skills in these digital writing spaces.

Thus, our focus should be that the students are actually reading and writing; we as the teachers just need to help them distinguish the difference between formal and nonformal writing. In fact, we need to help them understand audience, purpose, and situation. Kristen Turner has described the kinds of moves that writers make from a formal register to "digitalk" as a form of code-switching (Turner, 2009, 2012). Students' grammar, we should note, is also not being destroyed by BRB, gr8, and other forms of text lingo. If anything, researchers are showing that the transition between formal and txt speak is actually showing signs of greater linguistic competence (Kemp, 2010; Plester, Wood, & Bell, 2008).

Furthermore, the use of technology is showing improved student achievement due to the fact we are using tools that are easily accessible to students. They are able to stay in touch with others through RSS readers, social networks, e-mails, mobile phones, and other online tools. "Computer composition allows for multimedia components such as voice recordings audio, image, video, and more" (DeVoss, Eidman-Aadahl, & Hicks, 2010, p. 21). These compositions enable students to share their personal and academic lives in public spaces. Our students today have a plethora of options to express themselves as writers.

Creating a safe academic space for students should be at the forefront for any teacher using mobile devices in the classroom. By providing students a safe environment where they can express themselves freely within the perimeters of any school, the students can and will emerge as mature, responsible digital citizens. These are beliefs that our profession has held dear forever, even if we are just now moving into digital spaces. We can help in that transition.

Setting the Stage: Permissions and Sign-Ups

Prior to the start of school, we have an orientation night for the middle school students and their parents. Students visit their homeroom teachers, try their locker combinations, and do a shortened walk-through of their schedule. Parents attend a welcome and introduction by our principal, and they are introduced to teachers. We have about two to three minutes to introduce who we are and what we teach. Parents also get plenty of handouts from the office, athletic coaches, and teachers. This year the math teacher and I decided to hand out a CCSS parents' guide that is free and available online. The guides can be found at the national PTA Web site (National Parent Teacher Association, n.d.). In addition to giving parents a handout, I send out a newsletter once a month digitally via e-mail, and I post the newsletter on Schoology. I do provide hard copies to any family that does not have access to e-mail or the Internet.

Before we really dig deep into any unit, there are many logistics or what I refer to as housekeeping items. Taking care of these items sets the stage for the rest of the year. One of the first items I attend to is sending home opt out letters to parents with concerns to the types of technologies we will be using in class. The letter can be found on the resource website that accompanies the book (createcomposeconnect.wikispaces.com).

The reason I send home an opt out letter instead of a permission slip is easy. Along with the fact that my principal gave me permission to ask for permission in this manner, it is a huge time saver! I don't have to track down students who have not turned in a permission slip, and I don't have to make phone calls home to parents asking for permission. I also don't have to keep track of any papers. One less folder in the file cabinet drawer isn't a bad thing. In the past I used to send home separate letters for the different tools I would implement into my classroom; however, it is easier to have one simple, uniform letter for the parents to read.

The downside to an opt out letter is you don't really know if the student has taken it home. I cover myself by sending out an e-mail to parents, and I make mention of it in my monthly newsletter that goes home both electronically and via hard copy. Be prepared for a parent to sign the letter. This year I have had three letters returned out of the 120 that were sent home. I made contact with each one of these parents to discuss their reasoning behind not allowing their student to participate in the use of these digital tools. Though I didn't completely convince any of the parents to let their child participate, I still feel I planted a seed with the parents about the usefulness behind the tools we are using.

With any implementation, you are going to run into a few roadblocks. I need to take into consideration not only the few parents who don't want their children to participate, but I also have to consider the students who don't have access to mobile devices or the Internet outside of school. These circumstances aren't too difficult to overcome if I give students the choice on how they want to turn in certain assignments. Believe it or not, there are students who would rather write out a paper for me than type it. Unfortunately this does take me away from creating a paperless classroom. In addition to choice, I do go in early to school and stay later so students can utilize the computers in my room or perhaps jump on my iPad, which I bring into the classroom.

One additional note on acceptable use policies (AUPs): for a comprehensive review and recommendations about how to develop AUPs that meets the evolving needs of students, I encourage you to check out the Consortium for

School Networking's constantly updated guide titled "Acceptable Use Policies in the Web 2.0 and Mobile Era" (Consortium for School Networking, 2011).

Getting Started with Schoology

Standard SL.7.1: Engage effectively in a range of collaborative discussions (one-on-one, in groups, and teacher-led) with diverse partners on grade 7 topics, texts, and issues, building on others' ideas and expressing their own clearly.

After the letters are returned, we move forward, and the students get their Schoology account set up. Students do not need to register with an e-mail address for this social media Web site. All they need is the access code that is created when the administrator creates a course. When the students enter the access code, they are then allowed to fill the appropriate fields necessary to gain access. I require my students to use their last name and the first initial of their first name for a user name. For example, Hylerj. When the students create passwords, I encourage them to use a password they can recall easily, and I have them write it down. One of the nice features about Schoology is if a student forgets his or her password, the teacher can reset it. The Web site goes through a quick tutorial with new users. I then have the students watch a short video on YouTube about the uses of Schoology. In addition, I interact and collaborate with the students on Schoology by posting a quick discussion topic. Seeing how it is the beginning of the year, I do something that helps me get to know the students. Schoology also has a smartphone application students can download for free. Amazingly enough, by posting a discussion and interacting with my students online, I am already meeting the needs of the CCSS. Students are able to identify technology (Schoology) and collaborate with peers and their teacher through technology to enhance their writing.

Digital Writing with Schoology

With each tool introduced from here on out, I will outline the MAPS specifically for the digital writing tasks that I am asking students to do. Refer back to chapter 1 for a review of MAPS, and look for these boxes throughout the rest

Table 2.2 MAPS for Digital Writing with Schoology

Mode	Initial response to literature; additional response to other readers' interpretation
Media	Short, social network-style posts
Audience(s)	Teacher and peers (not available for outside visitors)
Purpose(s)	To demonstrate comprehension and analysis of text; to participate in conversations about the text and the themes that it raises
Situation	Time allotted in class, completed using computers, set number of required posts, set number of required responses

of the book to quickly identify the writing tasks I ask my students to complete. The MAPS for Schoology is shown in Table 2.2.

Sample Lesson: Thoughtful First Posts on Schoology

Standard 8.W.3: Write narratives to develop real or imagined experiences or events using effective technique, relevant descriptive details, and well-structured event sequences.

With my eighth graders, we did six-word memoirs, and I talked about making connections and creating a thoughtful response. The six-word memoirs are scaffolded into the student's bigger memoirs they do later. The eighth grade memoirs are discussed in chapter 3. Here are two student examples:

- Ate Mom's cooking; died right there! (Emily's six-word memoir)
- Keep smiling, even without the camera. (Madison's six-word memoir)

The trick here is to get students to do more than offer the standard one-word or other simple response. I want them to have an engaging conversation with a peer about the initial post. For example, they can't just say, "That's great!" Instead, they need to get to some slightly deeper questions such as, "What did you like most about this writing? What did it remind you of? What suggestions might you have for the writer? What questions still remain for you?" Schoology allows the writer and responders to engage in an ongoing conversation about the writing through a threaded conversation. The format makes it

easy for students to respond to and like one another's posts, much like they do on Facebook.

Getting Connected with Google Docs

In addition to Schoology, the students' set up their Gmail account for the use of Google Drive/Documents. This does not have to be a complicated process, especially if your school is already a Google Apps school. In my case, we just transitioned to using Google Apps, and I am confident saying that many of the teachers in my district aren't aware of the full capabilities of Google Apps. Districts can sign up for Google Apps for Education accounts at www.google. com/enterprise/apps/education/. However, I have my students register for their own account, with parental permission.

Once all of my students are registered for a Gmail account, I walk them through Google Drive and have them create a folder and label it seventh or eighth grade writing portfolio. This portfolio travels with them from seventh grade through at least their junior year in high school. As teachers, part of our teacher evaluation is measuring student growth. My district has agreed to use pre- and post-tests. In addition, our principal asked us to discuss within our departments what could be a third way to measure our student's growth. As a language arts department we decided to use writing portfolios/digital writing portfolios. By having students compile their writing into a portfolio, we can accurately measure how the student has grown over the course of a year and even over several years.

We also discussed if teachers should be measuring individual student growth from pre- and post-examples of their work or if we should measure them against a standardized objective. The argument that our department struggled with is how do we accurately measure from the beginning when students essentially start out with nothing? As individuals, we all grow differently as readers and writers. For example, I know I have grown more as a narrative writer because I was challenged to write this genre during the writing project. If students measure against themselves, they may see more growth in certain genres simply because they are weaker in that particular area. Despite the ongoing conversation that we continue to have, the goal is to show student growth in an effective manner. Below (Image 2.3) is a student example where a Google document has been used. The student received feedback on a short assignment and needs to go back and make corrections to the highlighted areas, thus showing some short-term growth as a writer through collaboration online. Like Schoology, there is a free app for smartphone users. We will revisit Google Docs throughout future chapters.

Image 2.3 Google Docs Screenshot with Comments and Highlighting

Table 2.3 MAPS for Digital Writing with Google Docs

Mode	The genres depend on the task at hand and can include the "big three"—narrative, informational, and argument—as well as note-taking, reflections, Q/A, or other interactive modes.
Media	Collaborative word processor allowing for simultaneous writing and editing; tracks user comments and revision.
Audience(s)	Google Docs allows for various levels of sharing: private, shared with selected users, shared with everyone. Also, these users can have privileges only to view, to comment, or to edit.
Purpose(s)	Like the mode, the purposes will vary depending on the task at hand.
Situation	Users can interact with Google Docs through a Web browser or the Google Drive app on iOS or Android.

Sample Lesson with Google Docs

Since there are so many possibilities for creating different modes, or genres, of digital writing with Google Docs, I will further explore the idea of MAPS in other units later in the book, but here are some general ideas in Table 2.3.

Texting and Tweeting

Finally, I have to get my cell phone users ready to use Cel.ly (Table 2.4). Cel.ly is extremely effortless when it comes to getting you and your students started.

Table 2.4 MAPS for Digital Writing with Cel.ly

Mode	Response to books via literature circle; journal prompts; reminders for homework; answering student questions; exchange of text messages between characters
Media	Group text messaging
Audience(s)	Teacher and peers (our "cells" are set up only for class use)
Purpose(s)	Depending on the particular mode, the purpose of the Cel.ly message varies
Situation	Even though they are texting, I still ask students to adhere to most grammatical expectations because they are responding to the entire class

Cel.ly does require you to create an account, and you, the teacher, will be the administrator of that account and all of the cells you create for your classroom. Cel.ly, in essence, is a private community that can be built by the teacher or potentially a student to exchange messages, send out reminders and alerts, or conduct polls.

There is nothing to download and anyone can use it. Cel.ly has a full Web console where students can still text from a computer while on the actual Web site, which means that everyone can participate, even those students who forget their phone or who do not have one. In addition, Cel.ly has an application for mobile devices on iOS and Android. The application is very similar to the Web version that can be accessed from a desktop or a laptop. The student's phone numbers are never exposed. The teacher controls all of the privacy settings. In addition, you can control the messages that group members see with a curate option that can be controlled by editing the settings within the individual cell that is created.

Here are a few quick but thorough steps to help any instructor get started:

- "Start" a cell—the name of the cell needs to be between 6 and 20 characters with no spaces. When I create a cell, I use the hour and my last name.
  - For example, Hyler3rdhour is my third-hour class, and if I want to send a message just to third hour, I can do so easily. I have three seventh grade classes and two eighth grade classes, and by organizing by hours, I can target each individual group more efficiently.
- Students will need to set up an account and a screen name for themselves. Encourage your students to use their real names and not nicknames. This

will help eliminate any confusion when it comes to assessment. Signing up is easy, as you can see in Image 2.4.

- Students will need to be invited to the cell. Cel.ly gives you three different options. A teacher can invite students by sending out a link privately or publicly. Cel.ly can also do it for you. It is best to do it privately, as the cell you are creating should be private and open to students or parents only. As the administrator of the cell you must approve the requests to join once the invite is sent. See Image 2.5.

Setting up takes no more than 20 minutes, and it does depend on the number of students who are using cell phones in your classroom. The greatest aspect about Cel.ly is that it is a free platform to use (standard texting rates do apply, however). Furthermore, there is nothing to download on a school computer or your own personal computer. In addition, even though smartphones seem to be slowly edging out simpler phones that only possess texting and calling capabilities, students who have access to any phone with a texting

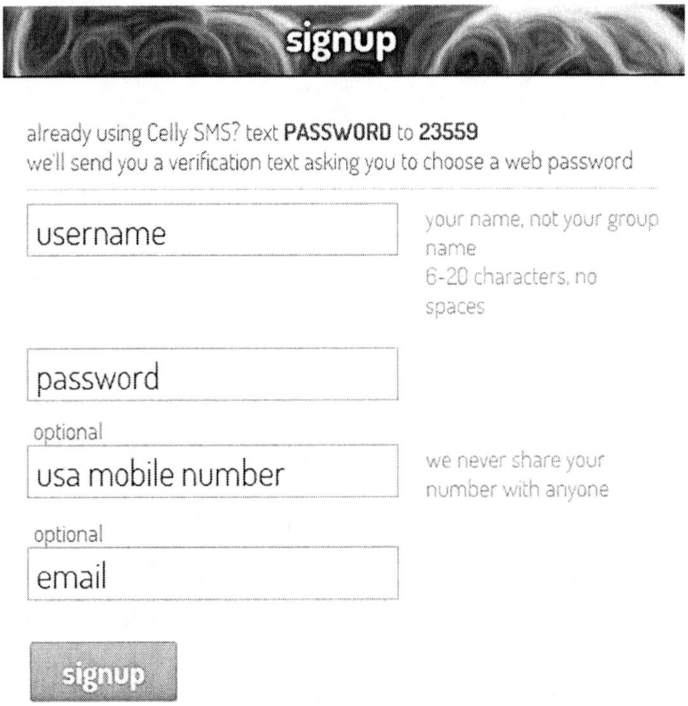

already using Celly SMS? text **PASSWORD** to **23559**
we'll send you a verification text asking you to choose a web password

| username | your name, not your group name 6-20 characters, no spaces |

| password |

optional
| usa mobile number | we never share your number with anyone |

optional
| email |

signup

Image 2.4 Screenshot from the Cel.ly Sign Up Page

best option - share golden ticket link

share this link via email, text, or post on facebook/twitter: | http://cy.tl/SghZuo

note: anyone with this link can join without your approval, so be careful posting it.

good option - text to join or share public link

or share this public link with members: | http://cy.tl/SghZum

note: If your cell is private, you will have to approve new members or they will need the password.

ok option - let Celly send invites for you

- This option is the least successful because it doesn't come directly from you.
- Members are less likely to trust a text or email from Celly.
- This option works well for inviting people who are already Celly members.

Enter **up to 100** email addresses, USA mobile phone numbers, or Celly usernames:

Image 2.5 Screenshot from the Cel.ly Invite Page

plan can still access Cel.ly. For more information, check out Cel.ly's great help guide at http://support.cel.ly/home

Middle school teachers should experiment and observe with a single class first, and then when you feel you have a solid understanding of the way a new tool works, start using it in more than one class. Last year, I made the mistake of implementing a new tool in all of my seventh and eighth grade classes (twice, actually). I overwhelmed myself by creating five cells for Cel.ly in all five of my language arts classes when I should have created a cell for one seventh grade class and one eighth grade class.

Then, as I worked through the bugs and fleshed out my guidelines, I could have created cells for my other three classes. The lesson learned on my part is to try it in one class first, then expand from there. However, I quickly forgot that lesson when I learned about Poll Everywhere (www.polleverywhere.com/) at a PD session, and I was so anxious to implement it into my classroom the very next day that I forgot my own lesson learned earlier with Cel.ly. Needless to say, since then, I haven't walked down the path of rushing into the use of technology.

Sample Lesson with Cel.ly

First, I have both seventh and eighth graders complete a basic journal response where students respond to a prompt I put on the cell, and then the students have to respond to two of their classmates. Below in Image 2.6, you will see a conversation on Cel.ly where students describe what the next scene might be in the graphic novel *BloodSong: A Silent Ballad* by Eric Drooker (2009).

Besides Cel.ly, I use the popular social media Web site Twitter in my classroom. Twitter allows me to not only communicate to my students, but they can communicate with their classmates. First, I want to make it clear I do not follow my students or even recommend they follow me. Again, I discuss with my students the importance of safety on social media Web sites. In addition,

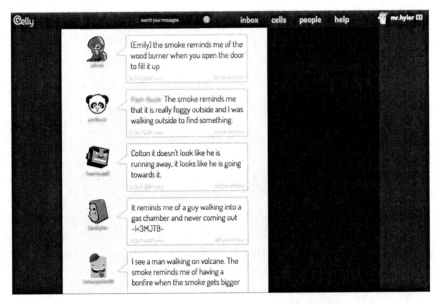

Image 2.6 Screenshot from the Cel.ly Discussion

I show my students how I use Twitter as a resource, not as a social playground for me to display my life to everyone. Instead of having students follow me, I use a hashtag (#) to create a key area or topic for my students to follow. For my classroom, I use the hashtag #HylerLA, so students can follow what is going on in my language arts class. It is also the hashtag where my students post tweets if we are doing a lesson for class. For example, I have my students complete a 140-character tweet about themselves as an introduction to the Twitter world. Before they post it to Twitter, they must compose a "paper tweet" as a rough draft of sorts before going live with their tweet. Below you will find Chole's example.

> Gathering the strength to climb, getting the courage to jump, closing our eyes as we fall. (Chole Delgado, eighth grader)

A Defining Moment: Using Apps to Support Reading Comprehension

Standard RL.7.4: Determine the meaning of words and phrases as they are used in a text, including figurative and connotative meanings; analyze the impact of rhymes and other repetitions of sounds (e.g., alliteration) on a specific verse or stanza of a poem or section of a story or drama.

A significant part of reading any type of text is asking students to learn new vocabulary. I use two tools hand-in-hand with each other on the mobile devices used in our classroom. I first introduce dictionary.com, a Web site that can be accessed easily through a laptop—or an app on a cell phone or tablet—when we read our first short story of the year. The eighth graders are already aware of it from the year before. It is the student's portable dictionary. Now, I have actual dictionaries in my classroom, but in the last three years, I think they have been used once. Students are more likely to access definitions for their vocabulary terms or words they do not understand in any reading by accessing their tablet or mobile phone. It really becomes useful when students are completing an article of the week for me throughout the year, which is discussed in chapter 5. Dictionary.com is a phenomenal reference tool for teachers and students. There is an iPad application, and it is available in the Google Play

Store. Because commercials and advertisements can potentially be distracting to students, Merriam-Webster has an application with fewer advertisements. However, if you want the luxury of a noncommercial app, an individual will need to pay around $3.99.

While dictionary.com serves its purpose on its own, when it can be paired with another tool, the two combined can create ultimate study tools for the students. I discuss with the students that they can work harder or smarter. I model for the students how to locate a definition and they can copy and paste it to a Web site called Quizlet.com. Quizlet is a free site where students can create online flashcards for studying purposes. Additionally, teachers can post flashcards there for students to access. There are also quiz features that can easily be created and printed off for tests or just checking for understanding (Image 2.7). Quizlet has an iPad application, but there is not an app on the Google Play store for those students who may be Android users. In addition to using the tool to complete vocabulary by itself, it can be used by the student who is responsible for vocabulary when participating in literature circles. I also encourage my students to use this tool beyond my classroom.

Image 2.7 Screenshot from Quizlet

Listening to Grammar Girl

To me, grammar is an enigma. The proper way to teach grammar to my students continues to elude me (if there is a proper way). I have read and researched Jeff Anderson (2005, 2007), Amy Benjamin and Joan Berger (2010), and Michael W. Smith and Jeff Wilhelm (2007). When it comes to teaching grammar in my classroom, I do not like to teach it as a stand-alone lesson. A teacher could deliver it a number of different ways. I try to tie it into what the students are writing and what we are reading in class. Hence grammar is taught repeatedly throughout the year.

Standard L.7.1

1. Demonstrate command of the conventions of Standard English grammar and usage when writing or speaking.
   a. Explain the function of phrases and clauses in general and their function in specific sentences.
   b. Choose among simple, compound, complex, and compound-complex sentences to signal differing relationships among ideas.
   c. Place phrases and clauses within a sentence, recognizing and correcting misplaced and dangling modifiers.

Standard L.8.2

2. Demonstrate command of the conventions of Standard English capitalization, punctuation, and spelling when writing.
   a. Use punctuation (comma, ellipsis, dash) to indicate a pause or break.
   b. Use an ellipsis to indicate an omission.
   c. Spell correctly.

For example, seventh graders are reading *The Acorn People* by Ron Jones (1996). The author uses sentence fragments for more effect. I spend time not only discussing sentence fragments, but we also do exercises with complex, compound, and compound-complex sentences. The eighth graders' first novel, *The Outsiders* by S. E. Hinton (1967), has plenty of dialogue. One of the requirements my eighth graders have for their first writing assignment, a memoir, is to create dialogue. We study the novel as our mentor text, paying attention to how dialogue looks in writing and the specific punctuation being used.

Before we dive too far into specific grammar, I like to get a sense of how well my seventh graders know the parts of speech. I am not huge fan of giving out worksheets when it comes to grammar or anything else. There are other ways to measure how much students know. For example, I have my students use Mad Libs to identify parts of speech. Who doesn't enjoy Mad Libs? There are even applications: Android has Pocket Mad Libs and iPad has Mobilibs. If you are simply using a mobile device such as a laptop, all you need to do is Google "Madlibs" and see which one works best for you. There are plenty of Web sites to choose from, including www.madlibs.com.

I personally like the ones that students can create and send to me through e-mail, and that way I am still keeping my classroom paperless. Besides doing this type of activity for a quick check for understanding, it keeps the students more engaged in grammar. In addition, the students produce funny and interesting stories to read and share, which is another great way to build a safe writing community. The students aren't so uptight and they have fun being silly.

Once the basic parts of speech have been covered, I move into my grammar lessons for this particular unit. As mentioned earlier, one of the areas of grammar I cover for seventh graders is the different types of sentences and, for eighth graders, how to effectively use dialogue. I accomplish this by using Grammar Girl (www.quickanddirtytips.com/grammar-girl). Launched in 2006, Grammar Girl is an educational podcast designed to give the listener tips and grammar exercises to help tackle all of the grammar, punctuation, and word choice rules.

I post the selected podcast link on Schoology, and the students bring their earphones to class and spend the first five to eight minutes listening to the podcast. I love Grammar Girl! It gives the students a chance to not only listen to the podcast, but they can also follow along on the written script. The students are afforded an opportunity to listen to someone else besides myself. Grammar Girl is free on a Web site called Quick and Dirty Tips. There is an app, which gives you easy access to all of her podcasts, for a mere $1.99. I bought it for my iPad in case I need to locate something quick for a student or our mobile lab is unavailable. At the conclusion of listening to the podcast, I have the students complete an individual activity and then a collaborative activity within their groups where they are seated.

First, the seventh grade students complete the following tasks for their grammar and vocabulary.

- Open a new Google document, and write out the definition of a simple, complex, compound, and compound-complex sentence in your own words.

- Next to each definition, write an example of each type of sentence.

- Share the document with Mr. Hyler for credit. Sharing a document gives the writer a number of options. Users can allow other collaborators to edit, view, or write comments. In addition, users can send a public or private link for people to view the document. As you can see, links can be shared via Twitter, Facebook, Google Plus, or e-mail.

Students then create folders within Google Drive. I have the students create several folders within Google Drive. Below are the folders I have my students create:

- Writing portfolio
- Journal entries
- Narrative
- Informational
- Argumentative
- Multigenre project

After their first task is complete, I have them work in their assigned groups. The students take turns sharing their definitions and their sentence examples. I walk around the room to assess when I feel that everyone is done; then I hand out dry-erase sentence strips with markers, and I assign each group a specific sentence type, which they must write on the sentence strip. For instance, group one would write a complex sentence on the strip. When all of the groups are done, each of them takes turns reading their sentence, and then I ask the other groups why it is, say, a complex sentence or how we can be sure it is an accurate example by the group. Image 2.8 is a picture of a few student group examples.

To keep things digital, I post the sentence strip activity on Twitter so students have access to multiple examples of each type of sentence. The sentence strip activity is a modified activity out of Jeff Anderson's *Mechanically Inclined: Building Grammar, Usage, and Style into Writer's Workshop* (2005). All of the activities are student directed, and I am merely a guide to what they have learned. The students stay on task, work hard, and enjoy grammar much more

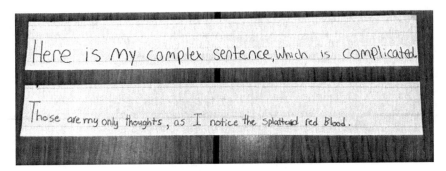

Image 2.8 Samples of Student Sentences

because they are not hearing me talk more, and it is not another boring worksheet for them to complete.

Conclusion

Whew! It sounds like a lot of class time has been lost by setting up the different digital tools and going through all of these lessons. I can understand that some colleagues would be concerned about the loss of precious class time, especially at the beginning of the school year.

Yet, if I were to calculate how much classroom time I actually used, it comes out to just about five class periods with my seventh graders. So, in the first two weeks, where we had all of this and other back-to-school work going on, this basically amounted to introducing them to the tools shared in this chapter. With the eighth graders, most of this is just review, and we spend much less time getting reacquainted with the tools and Web sites. Setting the stage for the use of digital tools on our mobile devices ensures smoother transitions during lessons throughout the units. As one of Troy's mentors used to remind him, taking time at the beginning of the year to establish relationships and create procedures will help later on. "You will take some time now, or take more time later" was his mentor's mantra. Take the time to set up the tools, in the right way, and it will lead to success for the rest of the year.

Still, I do not want to overwhelm the students or parents. To help ease any anxiety parents may have about the mobile devices or digital tools that are being used, my two colleagues and I hold a math/science/technology night. Parents are invited to see and personally experience what ways their child may use technology in the classroom. Additionally, the CCSS calls for improved rigor within our lessons. Adding technology is not only required by the standards but helps add that rigor. Students need to adapt to environments where multiple digital tools are being used. With a competitive global market and the ever-growing use of technology, it is imperative we use the devices that are at our student's fingertips daily and teach them the different media and modes that can be used.

Today, it isn't easy to reach our young readers and writers. Mobile technology is essentially at our student's disposal every day, and in reality they are reading and writing every day; they just happen to do it through different media. By using sites such as Facebook or technologies such as instant messaging, our students truly are being readers and writers. In addition, students are continuing to be connected to the Internet in some capacity. A study done by the Pew Research Center revealed that 93% of students ages 12 to 17 go online several times a day; additionally, 71% of teenagers ages 12 to 17 own a cell phone, and 97% of teens ages 12 to 17 play computer, Web, portable, or console games (Lenhart, 2009). The foundation of English and language arts is not changing, but the way our students are learning is. As educators we are responsible for shifting our thinking on how we do things in the classroom. We need to teach students how to be effective learners of English through these different venues.

What's Next?

Remember, there is nothing wrong with taking your time with integrating a technology into the classroom. It is more effective when the teacher has a solid grasp of the tool before delivering it to their students. There are a lot of tremendous digital tools that are enjoyable to use from the student's perspective as well as the teacher's perspective. Learning beside our students can deepen our understanding of the technologies being used; also, the number of tools may seem overwhelming. It has taken me almost three years to implement the tools I have discussed thus far. As mentioned at the beginning of this chapter, if any teacher takes the approach of implementing just 2 new digital learning tools into his or her classroom, over a span of five years, that teacher will have 10 new tools. So, let's begin exploring even more possibilities now with my narrative writing unit.

The Rest of the Story: Reading and Writing Narratives

The CCSS focus on three specific "text types" for writing: narrative, argumentative, and informational. We know that the tests want argumentative writing; we have been told for years that we need to teach more information texts, but kids like narratives. So, how do we begin? Well, for me, it still comes back to story.

This year is the first year I kicked off the school year by doing a narrative unit. I have it planned that my narrative unit will last anywhere from 10 to 12 weeks. Prior to this year, I was all over the curriculum map. I jumped around from standard to standard without any real direction. In the past few years I've wanted my classroom to flourish with technology, to have students be active learners, and to deal with the introduction to the new national standards. Although the CCSS addresses the use of technology in the classroom, there are still some missing questions with the implementation: Why am I using technology in my classroom? What is the purpose? How will I get students engaged? Furthermore, I needed a solid plan to implement, and that is when I thought about focusing on the three specific areas outlined in the CCSS: informational, argumentative, and narrative.

Narrative reading and writing is typically easier for students to handle than informational or argumentative. Speaking from personal experience, I know that all of us could tell our story of beginning a new curriculum, such as the CCSS, and how it can seem like a juggling act. It doesn't have to be, and in my experience as a middle school teacher, students typically enjoy narrative writing more because they are allowed to be creative when it comes to writing their own narrative pieces, whether it be a short story, a personal essay, a memoir, or any of the various forms of fiction, such as historical or science fiction. I know that there will be time to move into informational and argumentative writing later in the year. I build on each genre throughout the year, showing students that writing can possess narrative, informational, and argumentative qualities. Furthermore, by discussing each of these genres throughout the year, the students are exposed enough to them so they have a solid foundation for beginning their multigenre project, which is discussed in chapter 8. Your district may require something different, but I would encourage anyone to begin with story, because—as the old adage goes—we all have a story to tell. Here is mine.

It is no secret that the teaching of narrative, especially personal narrative, has dominated the field of writing instruction for a long time. I often wonder, if teachers are making rumbles about the CCSS due to their comfort level of teaching narratives and because of the shift to implementing more nonfiction. In particular, the anchor standard for narrative writing states that students will "write narratives to develop real or imagined experiences or events using effective technique, well-chosen details and well-structured event sequences" (Common Core State Standards Initiative, 2010) While I don't think that anyone ever intended to ignore informational or argumentative writing, so many of the leaders in our field have built the core of writing workshop instruction around narrative writing. Nancie Atwell (1998), Lucy Calkins (1994), Ralph Fletcher (1992), and many other writing teachers have taught us about the power of the personal story and how that can help a writer become more engaged and confident. Even in nonfiction, we recognize that there are opportunities to use narrative structures or literary devices, such as rhyme, rhythm, and repetition, to make a point.

Given the long history of studying narrative writing, there are a variety of ways to think about narratives—what they are, how they work, and the purpose they serve. I feel narratives are important for middle school students, because the students are on their own adventure of who they are as individuals. With that being said, I can't help but think about Gary Paulsen and the narratives he writes. Paulsen uses his own experience to create characters such as Brian in *Hatchet* to explain his own struggles in life and perhaps help young readers relate to the situations he encountered (Paulsen, 1987). I was an outdoor kid when I was growing up. I loved to hunt, fish, and camp. I still do to this day. Gary Paulsen's writing piqued my interest and gave me a mentor text to follow as I embarked on my own narrative writing assignments as a student.

In addition, when I was growing up, books such as *Tales of the Fourth Grade Nothing* by Judy Blume (2007), *Jelly Belly* by Robert Kimmel Smith (1982), and countless books by Beverly Clearly helped mold me into the reader I am today. Furthermore, I found comfort in 11-year-old Ned in *Jelly Belly* who was gaining weight and so was sent to a summer diet camp. I was a young man who was tall and skinny and was having trouble fitting in. *Dear Mr. Henshaw* helped guide me down the path of writing and love of English in general (Cleary, 2000). Making connections with narratives such as these allows us to compare ourselves to characters and the problems they face. This is what I did as a student and what I want my students to be able to do. By giving students the opportunity to write narratives, they can put themselves in those different roles throughout the stories they create as they try to find their own identity.

Can narratives help students see the values of writing and language arts in general? Absolutely! Today I look to Suzanne Collins, famously known for *The Hunger Games* trilogy (2008, 2009, 2010). As a teacher, I look to Collins's writing to help engage even my most reluctant readers and writers. Characteristics of her narratives include the protagonist being female, plots that have violence, and valuable life lessons. Collins captures a very broad audience of readers. I take advantage of her novels and use them as a guide to helping students to see one of the many ways narratives can be written, and I have used her novels as mentor texts for vivid detail and especially character development. Without texts such as *The Hunger Games* or any other narratives, students aren't going to become better narrative writers. Furthermore, with reading and writing going hand in hand, students who don't read quality narratives are not going to grow as readers either. Narratives are just part of the story.

In their book *So, What's the Story?: Teaching Narrative to Understand Ourselves, Others, and the World* (2012), Fredricksen, Wilhelm, and Smith outline three major types of narrative structures: narrative nonfiction for writing about one's self, narrative nonfiction as a type of literary journalism to write about other people, and imaginative narratives. They also argue that any of these forms of narrative can be composed as digital stories, including images, audio, music, and other forms of media. Fredricksen and colleagues believe that

> narratives help us understand and share where we come from. But it's crucially important to recognize that narratives help us set a trajectory for our futures and that they are especially important in helping us explore what is expected of us and how we might want to resist expectation. (2012, p.17)

Without a doubt, we want students to both see themselves, literally and figuratively, in the narratives that they write. Whether it is a personal story about their own history or future, or an imagined history or future with the characters that they have developed, I want my students to enjoy language arts. In addition, I want them to put forth the best effort possible, no matter what they are doing in my class.

In addition, I strongly feel there needs to be focus directed back to the creativity that encompasses narrative writing. *Out of Our Minds: Learning to Be Creative* by Sir Ken Robinson argues, "If creativity is to become central to our futures, it first has to move to the heart of education" (2011, p. 49). Students have been pressed for too many years to pump out five-paragraph essays that show nothing in the way of creativity. They must play with language, explore different text patterns, and work to be creative. By starting with narratives, I can revisit aspects of this unit throughout the year. In this chapter, I will focus on two types of personal narrative writing: the "This I Believe" essay and the memoir. Each of these narrative writing tasks invites my students to think carefully about craft and voice, and how to best reach an audience, and both tasks are enhanced by the technology that we use to help organize and present our ideas. In the later part of the chapter, I will share some strategies, including literature circles and the use of comics for retelling and response, that invite students to think deeply about narratives.

Throughout the year, students read an abundance of short stories and poems, but ultimately my unit revolves around the novels *The Acorn People* by Ron Jones and *The Outsiders* by S. E. Hinton. There are alternate methods on how I meet the CCSS. I encourage both elementary and high school teachers to think about how they could adapt some of the lessons being taught in my classroom. Still, this chapter will explore some strategies to meet narrative reading and writing standards using laptops and tablets and multiple digital tools to help enhance any narrative lesson or unit while meeting the needs of the CCSS.

To do so, I employ a writing workshop approach that allows me to differentiate my instruction where everyone, including myself, is writing, modeling, collaborating, and providing feedback to make everyone a better writer. As Jennifer Sharpe states, "When we share and respond to writing—peer-to-peer in small writing groups, peer-to-peer in partner response, or teacher-to-student in individual writing conferences—we are assessing and immediately using that assessment to improve writing" (2010). My students use their journals where they are writing on a daily basis and using the ideas from those journal writings to propel them into becoming better writers. Writing workshops also allow me to do more formative assessments with my students, conferring with them on their writing in process rather than simply providing summative assessments at the end.

With this approach, I can pull them in as readers at the beginning of the year with narratives. For example, as they develop relationships with one another and trust in the process of writing, my students are more likely to share a short story they have creatively composed than completing a written response to an informational article. Students tend to share more of their experiences and beliefs fresh off the thrills of summer vacation and the new experiences that await them in middle school. The next three sections of the chapter cover three types of narrative writing: "This I Believe" essays, memoirs, and digital stories.

"This I Believe" Essays

My seventh graders' first major writing event is a "This I Believe" essay (Table 3.1). I enjoy doing this particular piece in class because not only do I get the opportunity to get to know my students better, but it also allows students to write and discuss their own characteristics, both internal and external. One of the biggest challenges students face when writing narratives is developing well-rounded characters. This personal narrative allows students to explore their own "character" and teaches them to use sensory details that are often lacking in student narratives.

"This I Believe" originated in 1951 and ran for four years on the CBS Radio Network with journalist Edward R. Murrow. The show became popular again in 2005 with NPR's Dan Gediman and Jay Allison (http://thisibelieve.org). It encourages people to share individual beliefs and personal motivations. I first

Table 3.1 MAPS for "This I Believe" Essays

Mode	Personal Narrative
Media	Google Document, potential podcast, Youth Voices Web site (chapter 4)
Audience(s)	Teacher, peers, students from other grades and schools
Purpose(s)	To show readers what beliefs students have and how those beliefs are shaped
Situation	Students write the essay at the beginning of the year to show how their beliefs have molded them as individuals. These essays will be used later in the year as an introduction piece when there is collaboration between my class and another class in a different district.

saw this type of essay during the summer writing institute. One of the other teacher consultants did her teaching demonstration about how she uses "This I Believe" in her high school classroom, and I implemented pieces of that lesson into my own class. Anyone can simply Google "This I Believe" essays and find a treasure trove of ways to implement them into the classroom.

Brainstorming

To begin, the students visit the "This I Believe" Web site. The seventh graders start the writing process by composing a paper list in their writing journals of 15 to 20 beliefs they have. They take the list and make a word cloud for brainstorming. Wordle is a Web site where students can create word clouds (http://wordle.net). A word cloud is a visual representation of words to help display the importance of words. In this instance, it is the student's beliefs that I want to stand out for others to see. Using word clouds, such as those created by Wordle, is a creative way for students to begin the writing process.

Brainstorming can be one of the most difficult parts of the writing process. "Getting started" often eludes students, and although traditional bubble maps can still serve a purpose, word clouds can be created in less time and students can refer back to them continuously to spark ideas or they can change a topic more easily if they are having trouble at this stage of the writing process. Using a word cloud gives the student control over how his or her brainstorming appears, and as a teacher it gives me the chance to display a part of the writing process that typically gets swept under the rug because it can be messy and deemed less important than stages such as drafting.

Students use the laptops in class to access Wordle.net to complete this part of the writing process. Other options for creating word clouds include TagCrowd, Tagxedo, Tagul, Textivate, Word It Out, and Wordsift. In addition, there are word cloud–creating applications available for iPad. These are Tag-Cloud ($0.99), Cloudart ($0.99), and WordCloud (free). Find links to all of these on the chapter 3 page of the wiki (createcomposeconnect.wikispaces.com).

After creating their cloud, students narrow those 15 to 20 beliefs down to their top 5 and then to the 1 belief they will use to write their essay. The students print their word cloud for me to display in my classroom. In Images 3.1 and 3.2, you can see a collection of word clouds and a close-up in which I captured a student's computer screen when they were working on their word cloud.

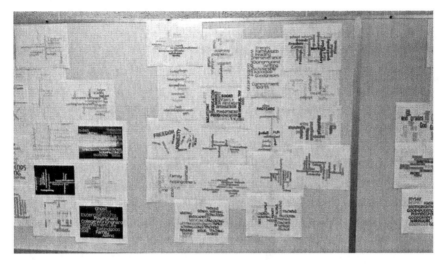

Image 3.1 Wordle Word Clouds

Image 3.2 An Individual Wordle Word Cloud

There are additional features of Wordle and other word cloud apps that can help students elaborate on their ideas. First, by adding a word more than once in a list, it will become bigger in the cloud. Students could, for instance, type in twice the one word that they feel is most important and all other words once. Also, students could take a chunk of text, like free writing, and then copy and paste to into the word cloud, which would then show them what words are showing up the most frequently. Second, students can change the font, color, and orientation of the words. By playing around with these features, they could create different moods that might reflect different approaches they could take in their final essay. Other word cloud sites allow students to manipulate the shape of the cloud, or the words within the cloud can show a relationship to the shape. For example, a science teacher might have students create a cloud in the shape of a heart with vocabulary terms associated with the circulatory system.

Authentic Models

Next, I have the students visit http://thisibelieve.org/themes. There are thousands of essays for the students to read and listen to as mentor and modeling pieces. I have the students bring their earbuds or headphones and instruct them to listen to and read along to three different essays of their choice. As they are doing this, they have their writing journals next to them and they list characteristics they find similar among the three essays. By doing this, they meet a speaking and listening standard for the CCSS (SL.7.2). When they finish, I give them all a link to a Google Document titled "Characteristics of 'This I Believe Essays.'" All of the students access the link I post on Schoology, and they began to feverishly type on the document while it is projected on the screen in my room. When students are done (I give them five minutes), we discuss all of the characteristics they find in common among the three essays by looking at what they have typed on the shared Google Doc link. Table 3.2 shows characteristics my third-hour class listed about the essays.

The class discussion leads us into the rubric for their essay because a majority of characteristics listed by the students are the same characteristics I look for when assessing their writing. I post the rubric on Schoology under files/links so the students have continual access. They can print it off at any time. During our discussion of the rubric, I ask the students if they notice the similarities between the characteristics they posted and what is listed on the rubric. Many faces light

Table 3.2 Characteristics of "This I Believe" Essays

Essay #1	Essay #2	Essay #3
First-person perspective Author states belief The words "I" and "me" are used 6 paragraphs	"I" and "me" are used Tells a story It is sad	Tells about belief The word "I" is used a lot Author has a lot of detail The author says "This I believe."

up and it starts to click that they already know what is required of them, and it isn't going to be too difficult to complete their writing assignment.

Drafting

At this point in the writing process, the students compose their rough draft on Google Drive. Students have already created their e-mail accounts, and I have walked them through how they use Google Drive. I show the students how to create a new document and folder. In addition, we walk through the process of sharing a document with not only me but also with their classmates. Google Drive allows students to access their document from anywhere there is an Internet connection, or students can access it from their cell phones or iPads. The collaboration component for Google Drive is incredible. In particular, the commenting feature allows students to respond to each other's writing and offer specific feedback on targeted sections of the writing. The learning can happen in the classroom, and beyond, when they give each other thoughtful feedback.

One major concern voiced by students and teachers is others writing on their shared document. I talk with my students about how the revision history can be reviewed, and if there is any sabotage to their writing, they would be able to see who wrote or deleted text on their document. Students can thus comment on their classmates' documents, and I require my students to share their writing with at least three other classmates for peer revision and editing. This is where the collaboration comes into play.

Revising versus Editing

Before my students can effectively collaborate and be efficient as peer editors or responders, it is important to have a conversation with students about the difference between revision and editing. As a writer and a language arts

Table 3.3 Revising and Editing Questions

Revising	Editing
1. Are there transitions present to tie key points together?	1. Are all words spelled correctly?
2. Can the reader see sensory details?	2. Is all punctuation correct?
3. Are the events you discussed in chronological order?	3. Are all verbs in the correct tense?
4. Has the writer eliminated statements such as "I am going to tell you about"?	4. Are capital letters present where needed?
5. Did the writer use seventh grade vocabulary and substitute dead words with appropriate synonyms? (For example: bad, sad, and mad)	5. Do all sentences have a subject and a predicate?

teacher, I know that there are differences between peer response and peer editing, and in my opinion it is crucial to teach students these differences. Revising includes adding and deleting detail. Furthermore, revisions can mean adding transitions and looking at the organization of one's paper. I discuss with my students about dissecting their papers and potentially moving parts of their paper around. One practice I like my students to participate in is to print off a copy of their paper, cut it into paragraphs, and move the paragraphs around to see if there is potentially a better order in which to organize the paper.

I think of editing as the students looking for spelling errors, capitalization, sentence structure, and grammar usage. Many students hear the term *peer response* and assume they just need to look for spelling, grammar, punctuation, and so on. I have my students complete editing and revisions during separate class periods. Students not only refer to their rubric but refer to a class-generated list of items for them to specifically look for in the writing they are editing and revising (Table 3.3).

Publishing

When students complete their final drafts, they share their work with me, and I provide my grade and comments right on the Google Doc. At the bottom of each student's writing, I embed the rubric with their score and grade for them to see. By having my students use Google Docs, they have helped me create a paperless classroom, and I am using a mobile application to help create a digital writing workshop atmosphere where my students are writing, revising, editing, and publishing together. Figure 3.1 shows what a final draft might look like, with my comments written in at the bottom.

Commitment

I'm 13 years old and like to have a good time. My favorite sport is soccer. I like to play other sports too. Some other sports I like to play are basketball and baseball. I'm good at school too. Sometimes, I wonder if it's a bad thing. Other times, it pays off. I also ref soccer, and I alter-serve at my church too.

First, it's hard to juggle all these things, but I still do it! With all my soccer games going on, after they are done, I have to go and ref soccer. I don't ref every game because some of my games run over the time limit. But this also means that I don't sit there and ref for hours on end. After I get done reffing, I get to get stuff for free at the concessions stand.

Next, I had to play my first soccer game of the season and ref. But this is, fun! We ended up winning 6-2! But the game ran over so I couldn't get to the game I was supposed to ref. A different ref was already reffing my game! I was a bit mad.

A few seasons ago, there was only one team that showed up for their game. I reffed. A senior ref told me to ask if they wanted to split their team and scrimmage. The coach accepted. So they won and they lost. The other team ended up showing up around twelve o'clock.

Another thing I am committed to is my schooling. I have earned plenty of A's in my life. I made it so if I got a C or lower on one of my report card, I wouldn't stop asking for extra credit until I achieved my goal. Luckily, I haven't had to worry about that it yet!

Basketball and baseball I don't have to worry about juggling with anything, but I need to work on basketball. This is the first year we have to try out. One time, I couldn't make free throws. Then, I had gone home. I decided to practice. I brought up our basketball hoop. It has been one of my best friends all year. Did I mention I couldn't make any free throws at school?

On the other hand, altar serving is one of my biggest commitments. Some altar- servers skip mass, at which they have to serve. I never skip. Well my mom makes sure of it. I have to go at least once a month. Usually I end up doing it three times a week. One time I did it a week then had to do it the next week too!

I've learned that you can do anything. That's my definition of commitment. If you try, you can do anything you set your mind to. Other times, it seems that when you committed, you feel like you can't stop no matter how tough you try. Now, I understand commitment is not what you do, its what you think you can do. If you lead a horse to water, try to make him drink. Commitment is when you don't give up on something because you know it is the right thing. It's when you say you're going to do something and do it. That is why I believe in commitment!

- Thesis - 4
- Purpose - 4
- Organization/Thesis - 4
- Details - 3
- Point of View - 4
- Writer's Craft - 3
- Conventions - 4

TOTAL - 26/28 A

Dear _____,
You did a great job since your rough draft. I am wondering if you could add more sensory details when you talk about your officiating and how you serve as an altar-server. As a reader I want to feel your excitement and commitment to what you discussed. In addition, we will need to continue to work on your voice and making that pop out of your writing. Keep up the great work!

Mr. Hyler

Figure 3.1 Final Draft of a "This I Believe" Essay with Comments

Memoirs

My eighth graders do some things similar to the seventh graders when they write a memoir that is more in depth than the "This I Believe" essay. Because I teach both seventh and eighth grade, the eighth graders already know what my expectations are for them in a writing workshop atmosphere. In addition, they know the high quality of work I expect of them. It is important for eighth graders to experience writing another personal narrative, because writing narratives often falls to the wayside with teachers at the high school level due to the extreme focus on informational and argumentative writing. I don't believe this is done intentionally, but rather it is done in order to focus on standardized testing such as the ACT, where students need to write an argumentative piece. Thus, students should continue to be exposed to the complexity of writing narratives before they enter high school.

Before the eighth graders write a complete memoir that consists anywhere from 4 to 10 pages (Table 3.4), I do a lot of scaffolding with them. We start with six-word memoirs, an original idea that comes from the online magazine SMITH (smithmag.net) and an idea I gathered from reading Kelly Gallagher's *Write Like This* book (2011). Here are a few student examples:

Going fishing soon (I hope so).

—Kanyon

Keep smiling, even without the camera.

—Madison

Table 3.4 MAPS for Memoirs

Mode	Personal narrative
Media	Word processer, Google Docs, digital voice recording
Audience(s)	Teacher, peers, parents
Purpose(s)	The writer will show effective use of narrative characteristics while writing about a specific experience in a given time frame.
Situation	Eighth graders will refamiliarize themselves with Google Drive and work on implementing enough sensory detail, which is an important characteristic when writing narratives.

Six-word memoirs have been done for many years, and I particularly like them because these could be adapted for elementary teachers, perhaps even as young as first grade.

In addition, the six-word memoir is a great starting point for students to start thinking in terms of an event in their life they want to talk about; it also demonstrates that writing doesn't have to be complicated to get a message across. There are many six-word memoirs filled with deep emotion despite the fact they are only six words.

After spending a class period with six-word memoirs, I begin the scaffolding process with my students. Next, the students write "Twitter Memoirs" or a memoir that cannot exceed 140 characters. Although I have used the Twitter platform in other ways, I adapted it this year as a scaffolding procedure like Gallagher explains in his book: "When introducing expressive and reflective writing to my students, I start them with something very light" (2011, p. 25).

By having the students produce a Twitter memoir, I am pushing them in terms of producing a lengthier piece of writing, but one where they have to get to the point. Twitter only allows 140 characters, and I explain to my students they have to decide what the most important ideas are that they want to convey in their writing. At times, I do find my eighth graders writing can be a bit wordy, and they don't get to the heart of what they are trying to say. Allowing them to only have 140 characters can help them to build on their previous six-word memoir by adding a piece of significant detail. In addition, it is still a lighter piece of writing that gets them into the mode of writing a memoir. Take Savannah's memoirs, for example, below. Her six-word memoir consisted of "Sports are my life; Volleyball, basketball." When she built on that in her Twitter memoir (which was 138 characters long), she was able to add more detail while getting straight to the point:

> Sports are my life. Volleyball, basketball, and softball. 365 days, every hour, every minute, every second. I eat sleep and breathe sports.

With students using Twitter, I have them use hashtags. For example, for the Twitter memoirs I could use the hashtag #FMSmemoirs. I have my students use the hashtag so they can place all of their memoirs into a common place where students can not only read them and give feedback, but they now have a place where they have some mentor texts as examples. It also helps the students see what others are thinking, and a student could potentially get ideas from what someone else has written. If teachers are not ready for students to access Twitter yet, the students can keep their tweets in their writing journals where they can easily locate them throughout the writing process. I call these paper tweets. On the other hand, they could compose tweets through Cel.ly, too, which was mentioned in chapter 2. Another student example (which is 137 characters), by Kara, can be found below.

> Korean, nice, respectful, loving. Friend, sister, granddaughter, great granddaughter. Always there, always listening, always your friend.

As the students begin to gain a better grasp on what a memoir entails, I share with them a very profound mentor text: *The Freedom Writers Diary: How a Teacher and 150 Teens Used Writing to Change Themselves and the World around Them* (Gruwell & The Freedom Writers, 1999). I read two or three of the shorter entries to the students and display them on a document camera. I invite the students to examine the characteristics of each. Students as writers are not going to be able to effectively write a narrative, or any other genre of writing, unless they can distinguish between the characteristics of narrative, informational, and argument writing. The book serves as another resource for my students to use when they are writing their bigger, more detailed memoir, which includes more events, characters, and complex emotions. I strongly believe the more models I can show my students, the better writers my students are going to become. My students spend a few more class periods writing and building upon previous writings.

Upon finishing these shorter memoir assignments, I hand out the rubric for the longer memoir. I give students time to read it, and we proceed by having a discussion about what they see and the important elements they are being graded on. In Image 3.3 you will see the rubric I use, which I adapted from a CCSS memoir rubric I found on the Web site of the New York–based Robert F. Wagner Middle School. For the most part, I kept the rubric the same. However, when it came to conventions, I was more forgiving in this area. I don't want the students to focus so much on the fact they are losing numerous points on grammar/conventions. I want them to worry more about their content as a whole when it comes to writing.

I give my students two days to get their memoir typed into Google Drive, and I give each student a formative assessment grade. With teaching both seventh and eighth grade, I don't spend a lot of time on reading rough drafts. Instead, I look at the rough draft in a formative sense and measure each student's ability and check to see if each individual student is writing to his or her ability. I do offer feedback on certain weaknesses that may pop out at me. This is easier to do with my eighth graders, because I have already taught them for

8th Grade Memoir Rubric (Based on Common Core Standards)
Writing Unit: Narratives

	4	3	2	1
Story Structure	• Memoir engages and orients the reader by setting out a problem, establishing a point of view, and introducing a narrator and/or characters • Create a smooth progression of experiences or events with a clear beginning, middle and end.	• Memoir engages the reader by establishing a clear setting and point of view. • The beginning introduces the narrator/characters and the problem. • The middle has a logical series of events that connect to the problem.	• Memoir engages the reader by establishing a clear setting. • The beginning introduces the narrator/characters and the problem. • The middle has a logical series of events that connect to the problem.	• Memoir begins by establishing problem. • The beginning introduces narrators/characters. • The middle contains events that connect to the problem, but they may not be in a logical order.
Narrative Qualities	Memoir uses a **variety** of narrative techniques to develop experiences, events, and/or characters, including: • Dialogue • Pacing (stretching one scene over another) • Sensory description • Reflection (inner thinking) • Multiple plot lines	Memoir uses **many** narrative techniques to develop experiences, events, and/or characters, including: • Dialogue • Pacing (stretching one scene over another) • Sensory description • Reflection (inner thinking)	Memoir uses **some** narrative techniques to develop experiences, events, and/or characters, including: • Dialogue • Pacing (stretching one scene over another) • Sensory description	Memoir uses **one or two** narrative techniques to develop experiences, events, and/or characters, including: • Dialogue • Pacing (stretching one scene over another) • Sensory description
Language Use	• Memoir uses a variety of techniques to sequence events so that they build on one another to create a coherent whole. • Use precise words and phrases, telling details, and sensory language to convey a vivid picture of the experiences, events, setting, and/or characters.	• Memoir uses a large variety of words, phrases, and sentences to show how the story moves from beginning to middle to end, and changes in time and place.	• Memoir uses a variety of words, phrases, and sentences to create a story that makes sense, with relationships clearly explained.	• Memoir uses words, phrases, and sentences to create a story that makes some sense, with relationships that are slightly confusing or may need further explanation.
Conclusion	Memoir provides a conclusion that follows from and **reflects** insightfully on what is experienced, observed, or resolved over the course of the narrative.	Memoir provides a conclusion that follows from and reflects insightfully on some of the narrated experiences or events.	Memoir provides a conclusion that may not connect clearly to the events, but still reflects on the narrated experiences or events.	Memoir provides a conclusion but may fail to reflect on the narrated experiences or events.
Conventions	Final draft had fewer than 4 errors in spelling, grammar, or punctuation. Dialogue is correctly punctuated.	Final draft had between 5 to 6 errors in spelling, grammar, or punctuation. Dialogue is correctly punctuated.	Final draft had more than 7 errors in spelling, grammar, or punctuation. Dialogue is mostly correctly punctuated.	Final draft had multiple (exceeding 10) errors in spelling, grammar, or punctuation. Dialogue is mostly correctly punctuated.

Image 3.3 Memoir Rubric (Used with Permission from Robert F. Wagner Middle School)

a year, and I have a solid grasp on each of their abilities based on their work and growth they made last year as writers.

Despite the fact I may not have a significant amount of time to individually conference with my students, I still make it my goal to spend 10 minutes a week with each of my students on his or her writing. It may not always be about the specific assignment we are working on, or it may not be as formal as conference time they have with me, but it still has an impact. Jay Mathews, an educational columnist for *The Washington Post*, stated in a column this past fall, "Just 10 minutes of editing a week per student does not seem like much, but such personal contact is powerful. By the end of a semester, that would total nearly three hours of personal editing per kid, unheard of in schools today" (2012).

In order for any student to take away or learn something from those 10 minutes, the meeting needs to be meaningful. As Lucy Calkins states in *The Art of Teaching Writing*, "Conferring is the heart of the [writing] workshop" (1994); numerous other teachers agree (Burke, 2003; Gallagher, 2011; Graves & Kittle, 2005; Kittle, 2008). I ask my students to come to their individual meeting prepared and ready to talk about their writing. My students have three questions they need to answer prior to our conversation:

1. What is the strongest part of your paper and why?
2. What is the weakest part of your paper and why? How can we work together to make it better?
3. What is one specific area in your paper you want Mr. Hyler to review? (For example, specific detail, dialogue, conclusion, etc.)

I create a Google Form and send it out to each of my classes via Google Groups. Google Form can be used to create surveys or quizzes or to collect other information. In this case, every student must respond with his or her name and answer the three questions. The students must fill out the form and submit it back to me the day before their conference with me. This allows time for me to look at what each individual need might be, and it gives students time to reflect on their writing at this stage in the writing process. Furthermore, the form helps to keep the meeting moving along. Each individual meeting last three to four minutes, and I feel confident the feedback is valuable to the students while helping them grow as writers.

When the eighth graders are done meeting with me, I spend time reviewing with them how to make comments and feedback on Google Drive. I go over how to insert comments, highlight text, and change text color to show the writer where revisions or editing needs to be done. I either have my students share with two other students or I put them into small groups for them to work on revision and editing. When a student gets done sharing his or her writing, it begins to looks like the example in Image 3.4.

By the time the students get done collaborating and they have had some practice doing it, I get pumped! Seeing the student's interact using their laptops while they are reading each other's papers is energizing. They are engaged and

days to get there, but to the rest of my family

vere just about halfway through Ohio the

that it needed to blow fuses which meant we

e charge any of our cell phones. So we stopped and

hey could fix them, but guess what? The fuses

ly we had sat there for those three hours of

ng accomplished. On the brighter side of things

at bad compared to the beginning of the trip. The

thing;drive, eat, stop at hotels, and then it would

essarily think my parents liked the car ride either

say "Are we close yet?", and they'd say "NO!!!!".

estination, things weren't as "peachy" as I had

el, the magnificent sight that we had seen online

nelling, people talking in accents I couldn't even

e to make matters worse, we had to stay there at

Image 3.4 Google Docs with Comments

generally enthusiastic about not only going over a classmate's writing but also the feedback they get on their own writing.

> I like Google Drive because when you write a paper or poem or anything on there it gets saved automatically. You don't have to search through all of your saved files to find stuff. I like that you can share your writing while you write it. I also like that it's easy to edit stuff on Google Drive.
> —Caleb

> Things I like about Google Drive are that you can access it on any computer or Internet device. I like that I have the choice of doing a blank document, a spreadsheet, a PowerPoint, etc. I like that you can just share your document with more than one person and you don't have the individually email it to each person.
> —Jourdan

After students have revised and edited their documents, I give them a 55-minute class period to polish their writing and share it with me through my school Gmail account. All of my comments and feedback are written directly on each student's document, which has been shared with me. Below is Savannah's memoir of a trip she took to Florida to see her sister who plays softball in college. The idea to write this memoir sprouted from the tweet she wrote that was mentioned earlier in this chapter. Savannah is the youngest of three siblings who have all played sports. Her sister was fortunate enough to be recruited for college, and the Florida memoir (Figure 3.2) is a solid example of how much she progressed from her tweet. In addition, it shows how committed her family is to sports.

Savannah's memoir is not the only memoir that was written well. I enjoyed witnessing the blossoming my students did from their original ideas. What I enjoyed even more was that I have not put a single paper in my school bag to carry home, and I can grade and give students feedback much quicker, especially since I can access Google Drive on my cell phone, laptop, or tablet anywhere I go and have access to wireless Internet service. Many times while I sit in the dentist or doctor's office, I can get two or three papers graded. This past fall when I presented at the National Council of Teachers of English (NCTE) in Las Vegas, I was able to grade complete class sets of papers while waiting for my flight. The work is still there, yes, but for some reason it doesn't feel as daunting.

When I am finished grading the students' papers, I spend some time discussing what their strengths and weaknesses are in this particular piece. I extend this piece of writing further by requiring the students to either create a video recording of themselves reading their memoirs or produce an audio recording, such as a podcast. "As a multimedia composing process, podcasting allows writers to use the power of tone and inflection, blending tracks and adjusting volume to create just the right effect" (Hicks, 2009, p. 71). Chapter 6 discusses speaking and listening with the CCSS in more detail.

High school teachers might consider voice recording their comments and concerns when they are grading their students' papers. This helps the students to develop listening skills and addresses the idea of formative assessment and creating differentiated instruction for each student. Jim Burke describes how a teacher can use a digital recording tool on the Internet or use a digital recording device to record feedback and then upload it as an attachment to an e-mail (Burke, 2013).

Florida

This year my Mom, Dad, and I went to the city of Kissimmee in the sunshine state of Florida. We went there for spring break to visit my sister because she had spring training for her college softball. Even though it was a rather long trip, it was probably the most fun vacation I've ever had. Except for the beginning . . .

Even though the trip turned out to be nice in the end, the car ride there was TERRIBLE! It took us three or four days to get there, but to the rest of my family and I it felt like forever! When we were just about halfway through Ohio the wonderful car that we own decided that it needed to blow fuses which meant we couldn't charge our GPS nor could we charge any of our cell phones. So we stopped and waited at a nearby mechanics until they could fix them, but guess what? The fuses . . . never ended up working! So basically we had sat there for those three hours of wasted time in my life, and got nothing accomplished. On the brighter side of things though the rest of the ride wasn't that bad compared to the beginning of the trip. The rest basically consisted of the same thing; drive, eat, stop at hotels, and then it would just start all over again. I don't necessarily think my parents liked the car ride either because every couple hours or so I'd say "Are we close yet?", and they'd say "NO!!!!". When we had finally arrived to our destination, things weren't as "peachy" as I had expected them to become . . .

When we finally got to our hotel, the magnificent sight that we had seen online turned out to be a crappy, cat pee smelling, people talking in accents I couldn't even understand kind of a place. Of course to make matters worse, we had to stay there at least for the first night because they wouldn't refund us for that one freaking night! When we had finally got out of that hotel the second day, things began to fall into to place and become much better.

On the second day things seemed to finally be working out pretty good. To start off we found a gorgeous hotel that had three pools, two hot tubs, continental breakfast, really comfy beds, AND wi-fi! Also, our hotel was right next to where my sister was staying with her team in a group of condos. So, if she wanted to visit she could just walk over to our hotel. Each morning my family and I would wake up and go down stairs to the breakfast area. As soon as we stepped through the door, various smells would linger under our noses. Those smells included pancakes, waffles, bacon, eggs, oatmeal, fresh fruit, and multiple kinds of juices. It tasted AMAZING! Then each day after breakfast we would head off to watch my sister and her Trine softball team do what they do best . . . play softball. After the games were done we would usually go out to eat at a restaurant then return shortly after to our hotel where we would take an evening swim our use what was left of the sun to get a nice tan. So basically we had the same schedule for the next five to six days or so, but then we got a free day where the girls didn't have a game so my dad and I came up with the genius plan of going to Disney Land.

When it was about five days into the trip, my dad and myself decided to go to Disney Land. As soon as we walked through those gates, I knew that day would be a memory I would never forget. Just like I had predicted it was! The first thing we did was go to a 4-D Shrek movie, which was AMAZING!!! It sprayed water, blew air, and much more. We also went to many more rides and entertaining things that were so much fun! In some of those rides there was fire, mummies, twisters, more fire, water, and complete darkness! In Disney Land there was even a whole room dedicated to the television show "I Love Lucy" which is one my favorite shows. In it was outfits that Lucy wore, a mini design of the set, and facts about the actors that starred in the show. Of course with every amusement park there are gift shops and the one we went to was really interesting. It had tons of stuff in it and everything was SO cool! There were only a couple of roller coasters, but just like all the other rides they were crazy good. Except for one ride, which was a Simpsons ride that I'd never do again, because it made my dad and I both feel sick! That was literally the only bad ride though because I enjoyed all the other ones a lot. All fun things must come to an end though and on that day they did and we had to go back to our hotel.

The next two days were our last days in Florida sadly and then we had to be back on our way home. The car ride back was sadder than it was boring and long. I hated saying goodbye to that state and I definitely hope to go back again. I had a blast in Florida from the nice tan I got, to going to Disney Land and I don't regret going at all. On the way home though I guess I had some fun. We stopped and saw the ocean, and i picked up a lot of seashells. What I forgot though is that the ocean's different from Michigan's lakes. For example in the ocean that I was just about up to me knees in there's jellyfish, sharks, stingrays and MANY more dangerous things that could harm me and of course I completely forgot about them. Then I stopped and thought to myself . . . I'm not in Michigan's lakes I'm in the ocean! By the time I realized that my mom called out to me," Savannah don't forget about the sharks and just be careful." So then I just plain old got out of the water because I didn't really feel like dealing with those things. Finally we were back in the car for the next couple of days and then back home. The beginning of the trip might of started out bad, but in the end I really enjoyed my spring break in Florida and hope to return soon.

Figure 3.2 Final Draft of a Narrative

Digital Stories

I was first introduced to digital stories (Table 3.5) when I attended the summer institute in 2010. Digital stories allow the students to use aspects of narratives while using videos, pictures, music, and text. It also uses storyboarding, where students will need to revise and produce a digital piece of writing, which is part of the writing process. My first impression of this activity was that it was going to be extremely time consuming and perhaps difficult for students to complete, but I saw the value. In *The Digital Writing Workshop*, Hicks states,

> Creating digital videos—like creating photo-essays and podcasts— requires that writers begin the process with a clear sense of mode and purpose, as well as an understanding of what they need to learn about particular technologies in order to build their final projects. (2009, p. 77)

Yes, this project takes practice and patience from both the student and the teacher. I am not trying to discourage anyone from participating in the brilliant creations that can come forth, but I just want to set a realistic stage for any teacher who has not had any experience with this activity. For more resources on digital storytelling gathered by teachers in the Chippewa River Writing Project, visit: http://chippewariverwp.wikispaces.com/digital_story telling. Also, Alan Levine has a great collection of digital storytelling resources at: http://50ways.wikispaces.com.

When considering the use of digital stories, there are a set of questions I found on Richard Byrne's blog site, Free Technology for Teachers. Byrne (2013) suggests we ask eight important questions, and with the exception of the last question referring to equipment, I revisit them every time we begin a digital video project such as digital stories.

Table 3.5 MAPS for Digital Stories

Mode	Personal narratives
Media	Images, pictures, drawings, music, text
Audience(s)	Teacher, peers
Purpose(s)	To create a narrative story digitally
Situation	Students will need to learn how to import media, add music and text, and then effectively put the various elements together.

- What do you want students to demonstrate?

- What is your knowledge of the creation process?

- What is your students' level of knowledge of content?

- What are your and your students' skills in writing, research, editing, assembling?

- How much time can you allot to this project?

- What are your skills? (Tip: do the project yourself from scratch)

- What are your students' skills?

- What kind of equipment do you have at your disposal? How often can you access that equipment? (Byrne, 2013)

In addition to the set of questions to help guide the project, there are also several objectives I set forth for my students when they create this unique kind of multilayered narrative.

- Think about audience to help shape writing.

- Integrate technology into the CCSS writing curriculum.

- Explore the voice of the students more.

- Create connections to digital literacies such as narratives with the potential for future connections with informational and argumentative writing.

- Be creative by using different medias.

Upon beginning the process of creating their digital story, I allow students to choose their topic. More times than not, students fall back on their "This I Believe" essays or their memoirs. Sometimes I have students go back through their journal entries in the folder they created in Google Docs and get ideas from previous entries. I must be diligent in making sure the students understand that their videos have to tell a story. In other words, the videos need to be narratives, with characters, plot, setting, and a conflict. On a separate note, my seventh graders create public service announcements (PSAs) during our argumentative unit; I will discuss the PSA project in chapter 4.

In addition, it is important to address fair use policy. During this time it is a good idea to talk about fair use policy and copyrighted material with your students. *Copyright Clarity: How Fair Use Supports Digital Learning* by Renee Hobbs (2010) is an excellent resource; I recommend it for all teachers. Hobbs explains the use of copyrighted material in plain English. "At the heart of copyright law, the doctrine of fair use states that people have a right to use copyrighted materials freely without payment or permission, for purposes such as criticism, comment, news reporting, teaching, scholarship, and research" (Hobbs, 2010, 18). Though it is difficult for students to discern the difference between fair use and infringement, students need to know who to give credit to when including something into their stories from the Internet.

In terms of the requirements you set out for your own students, the criteria can be determined however you would like. The differences I have for my seventh and eighth graders are the number of minutes their story needs to be and what elements need to be present in it. I give my students, both seventh and eighth graders, a two-week time window to complete their digital story. The two weeks break down like this:

- Day 1: Introduction to storyboarding
- Days 2 and 3: Students complete storyboarding
- Days 4 and 5: Fair use and gathering of resources
- Day 6: Introduction to Animoto and WeVideo
- Days 7 through 10: Creating and producing the digital stories

The students have two class periods to complete their storyboard. Upon approving their storyboards, I give feedback and suggestions to the students to help them improve the quality of the story they are trying to create. I stick with the basic idea of making sure there is a beginning, middle, and end. Furthermore, is the student truly telling a story? The students should have a script written, and there should be a clear purpose to the story. I also examine the storyboards for content such as what audio components are they going to use, what pictures, or what Web sites. Remember, the storyboards are the rough drafts, so they do not need to be perfect. Also, it's important to note that there are numerous Web sites and apps that will help students in the process of storyboarding; they're all listed at the end of this chapter. An example is shown in Image 3.5.

When I hand the storyboards back to the students, I give some brief reminders about gathering resources (chapter 8 discusses validating sources). Students bring in their cell phones, iPods, and so on to provide any music they may want for their story. I let my students know they are responsible for putting appropriate materials in their digital story. For example, they are not allowed to use music with explicit lyrics or include images of people that are too revealing.

Image 3.5 Storyboard

When students are ready to utilize their resources and put their stories together, I introduce WeVideo (www.wevideo.com) and Animoto (www.animoto.com) so the students can compose their digital story. Animoto is a Web application that produces videos that can include photos, video clips, and music. Using Animoto is free for 30-second video clips, but beyond that the site requires you to pay for the premium service. The site is very user friendly, with a video tutorial on the Web site; you can also find tutorials on YouTube, thus making it great for my seventh grade students. WeVideo is also free, but it is more complex to use. I typically direct my eighth graders to WeVideo because they have more editing options with WeVideo (see Image 3.6). Similar to Animoto, WeVideo provides tutorials for the students to watch that are very helpful. I find it helpful if you give students time to play around on the Web sites. The more they play with the tool, the more comfortable they will become and the easier it will be for the students to complete their projects. If you are fortunate enough to have iPads at your disposable, there is also the Storykit app, which is free. You can record sound, add pictures and simple drawings, and so on, just like any other venue where a digital story can be put together. Typically, students compose digital stories that last between one to two minutes. There are occasions when they run over, and I don't mind. I push my eighth graders to complete a two-minute video.

Image 3.6 WeVideo Interface

Part of putting the entire story together includes adding narration. I give the students a few different options when it comes to narration. I prefer my students to use Audacity (http://audacity.sourceforge.net), which is a free, easy-to-use audio editor that students can use right on their laptop. Also, digital voice recorders are fairly inexpensive and can be bought at most electronic stores, or students can use their phones. Audacity users must convert their recording to an MP3 file so it is compatible to use with platforms such as WeVideo. If the student elects to use a digital voice recorder, he or she must upload the sound file to his or her computer.

Music, pictures, text, drawings—all of these are important elements for a digital story; I outline a number of questions that I ask my students about each type of media in the following table (Table 3.6). Before we even begin discussing specific elements, I ask, "What do you think about these different media elements? How do you search for, find, organize, and integrate them into the digital stories? When is it best to compose your own media, or do you just find existing media?" Editing the final project—making the pictures change at the right moment or matching the narration to the pictures—is always a challenge. I recommend setting aside at least one class period when you can be free of any other responsibilities but helping students polish their stories. Students e-mail me their stories as attachments when they are finished.

Table 3.6 Questions to Guide Media Selection for Digital Storytelling

Music	Pictures
• Is the music meant to be background music or a part of the narrative? • What kind of emotion do you want the music to portray? What kind of instrumentation and musical genres would best convey that emotion? • How does the music relate to your own experience as well as the experiences of your audience(s)?	• How is the picture framed? How does the photographer portray the subject? • What kind of conclusion do you want drawn from the pictures that you are using? • If you use a copyrighted image, are you using it in a "transformative" manner?
Text	Drawing
• Are you using the text for a transition, or are you using it to tell part of the story? • How can we use the power of words to our advantage? For instance, with onomatopoeia, do you want to use text or sound effects?	• Typically, drawings are more personal and take you time to create; does that contribute to the story behind the image? • What kinds of feelings are portrayed in the image?

When assessing student projects, I use a rubric generator site for digital stories called DigiTales. The site allows you to create your own rubric no matter what type of digital story you want your students to create. I chose the short story rubric creator because I am pushing my students in the area of narratives, and I want them to replicate the elements of a narrative. You can find the link to the Web site on our book's companion wiki (createcomposeconnect.wikispaces.com).

To wrap up this project, I take a day with my students, and I allow them to bring in candy, popcorn, pop, and any other goodies you may find at the movies. This was something we did at the summer institute I attended for the Chippewa River Writing Project. Essentially we have a storytelling day: the students share their digital stories, and we feast on our treats while being an audience for each other. The students really enjoy this, and by eighth grade, they are excited when they know storytelling day is quickly approaching.

What's Next?

Narrative writing is just as complicated to teach our students about as informational or argumentative writing. Throw in technology, a multitude of digital tools, and the implementation of a national curriculum, and our heads seem to be in a never-ending spin. Focusing on story, and the particular elements of story, can help slow us down, refocusing our attention on important elements that go into developing narrative. When we invite students to explore stories—based on their own experience and imagined story worlds—we help them move through the creative process. After this, I then turn my students' attention to informational text.

Reading Our World, Writing Our Future (Informational)

The CCSS's focus on informational reading and writing should come as no surprise to educators. Informational writing goes much further than students cracking open their textbooks. Students may appear disinterested in informational reading and writing, but in reality they are more likely to gravitate toward it, and they have solid knowledge of the world of informational text.

At the beginning of my informational unit, I create a public document on Google Drive where students can contribute specific examples of informational reading and writing. Their list has included such items as magazines, almanacs, textbooks, billboards, newspapers, atlases, letters, daily school announcements, e-mails, Facebook posts, and text messages. One of the many conclusions I draw from the list composed by my students is they can identify different types of informational text. Furthermore, they do have some knowledge of what it means to write something that is informational. As we continue to focus on "career and college readiness," understanding the variety of genres and purposes related to informational texts is important. Even though the nondescript terms *paper* and *assignment* are often used to describe the types of writing that happens in high school and college, I want students to understand that informational texts can function in different ways, for different audiences and purposes.

Knowing my students do have some prior knowledge of informational text, it can be concluded they are exposed to it on a daily basis, perhaps without even being consciously aware. Now, I need to be creative in my own planning when it comes to assignments and activities within the informational unit that I teach them. I made a decision two years ago that I was going to teach beyond the typical compare/contrast essay that seems too prevalent in classrooms. Throughout this chapter I will be focusing on specific assignments

I have my students complete. These assignments—including my adaptation of Kelly Gallagher's article of the week, book reviews, and myths—give them insight into the world of informational reading and writing.

Article of the Week (AW)

RIT.8.6—Determine an author's point of view or purpose in a text and analyze how the author acknowledges and responds to conflicting evidence or viewpoints.

RIT.8.2—Determine a central idea of a text and analyze its development over the course of the text, including its relationship to supporting ideas; provide an objective summary of the text.

RIT.8.3—Analyze how a text makes connections among and distinctions between individuals, ideas, or events (e.g., through comparisons, analogies, or categories).

I first read about an article of the week on a plane when I was heading to Kansas City, Missouri, for a workshop. I read about it in Kelly Gallagher's *Readacide* (Gallagher, 2009). The idea behind an article of the week is for students to read informational articles taken from reliable sources such as magazines, newspapers, or Internet venues. The students read the article and "interact" with the article, which means they highlight, underline, ask questions, and make comments in the margin. Gallagher's Web site (http://kellygallagher.org/resources/articles.html) has articles he has used in his high school classroom.

While adapting this for middle school students, teachers will need to check the difficulty of the article chosen from the Web site to make sure it is grade level appropriate. As a resource, I use the link http://vms.vale.k12.or.us/articles-week, which is part of Oregon-based Vale Middle School's Web site. Anyone is free to use the Web site as long as credit is given to Vale Public School and their teachers, and, of course, Kelly Gallagher for the work put into AW. In addition to the reading, students have a written assignment for the article that can be adjusted for any level. The MAPS for AW is shown in Table 4.1.

I was compelled to implement this into my curriculum, but I knew I had to go further than just reading about it in a book. Teaching in a very rural district, I feel my students are in this proverbial "bubble," where all they care about

Table 4.1 MAPS for Article of the Week

Mode	Annotation, summary, purpose, intended audience, opinion
Media	Google Doc
Audience(s)	Teacher, peers
Purpose(s)	Students will demonstrate close reading of an informational piece of text and show understanding of what the author's purpose was for writing the article. In addition, students will show they can form their own opinions on given topics.
Situation	Students have an article of the week due every week. The article is e-mailed to them, and they are to complete the article assignment via Google Docs.

is what goes on in the hallways with the latest gossip or what is happening at home. My students need to take the time to figure out what is going on in the world around them. Needless to say, I was eager to bring the idea to our next department meeting, and I was thrilled when I found out one of the high school teachers had already made this a part of his weekly activities. After an in-depth discussion within our department, I was ready to proceed with implementing AW into my classroom.

When I first tried to introduce an article of the week in the second semester of the 2011–2012 school year, it flopped. Not because of what the students did, but because I failed to follow through and assign it weekly. I started out with the thinking that it would be one more assignment I would have to grade and one more set of papers I would need to cart back and forth to school.

For this past year, I made a few major overhauls on how I was going to use this in my classroom. To begin, I have gone digital with the whole assignment. When I first tried it, I handed out individual articles to the students along with a rubric, and we went over the procedures to make it better. I felt this was a waste of paper and a waste of resources. I am now sharing the article with each class via Google Groups. This requires me to create a group for each class and enter each student's e-mail address in order to share documents. Google Groups allows me to do much more than e-mail my students articles of the week. It can be used to send students links, homework reminders, assignment requirements, and so on. If students are absent I can do a screen capture of an assignment and e-mail it to them so they can see what is required of them upon their return. In addition, when I assign an article of the week, I date it, and each one is numbered for quick reference for missing, late, or absent work needing to be made up. I even put what marking period or term it has been assigned.

Students have one week to complete the assignment. For example, I assign seventh graders an article of the week on Tuesday, and it is due the next Tuesday. Again, I remind my students the importance of reading informational text and stepping out of their "middle school bubble." There are a lot of events going on in the outside world that can potentially have an impact on them now or in the future.

Furthermore, getting my students to think critically is also one of my ultimate goals with an article of the week. I want my students to challenge the ideas or form an opinion about the article. The point of students pushing back against the article is important because students need to understand articles can be potentially biased, and they should not always take what they see in the media for face value. There are multiple times my students have these "OMG" moments while they are reading the articles, and these moments can be not only the times they may question or disagree with the article but also times they have learned or been informed about a topic in which they otherwise may not have had any prior interest.

One particular article I had my students read was about the effects of drinking energy drinks such as Monster. The conversation that took place upon returning those articles was astounding. Most of my students had no clue the impact those drinks had on their body, and they were clueless about younger people who have died from ingesting too high of volume of energy drinks. I strongly believe some of my students stopped drinking energy drinks that day. Here is just part of the conversation, recreated here for illustrative purposes:

Mr. Hyler: "So what are your thoughts on this particular article you had to read?"

Kanyon: "I was surprised it led to so many health issues."

Sam: "Yeah, can energy drinks really cause your heart to stop?"

Mr. Hyler: "I am not completely sure, but perhaps if you drink too many it could throw the rhythm of your heart off to an extent."

Madison: "I don't completely agree with the article, I think the author was more concerned with the outcome of her own children drinking energy drinks."

Mr. Hyler: "Good Madison, I want you to form your own opinions; that is part of the reason we do article of the week. We shouldn't take everything we read for face value."

Another piece we read was about students and their use of Facebook.

Number is 150—well, 147.8, plus or minus. "Partly it's a cognitive challenge just to keep track of more people than that," Dunbar has explained. "And it's a time-budgeting problem: we just don't have the time in everyday life to invest in each of those people to the extent where you can have a real relationship."Dunbar's Number was calculated pre-Internet, but it applies to social networks, too. A study conducted in 2009 for The Economist found that people with 500 Facebook friends had actual interaction—such as leaving comments on people's walls or "liking" their links or photos—with an average of just 17 friends for men, 26 for women. And one-on-one communication, such as individual messages or Facebook chats, was even more limited: men had two-way contact with an average of just 10 of those 500 friends, women with just 16. Facebook itself has figured this out and has developed an algorithm that restricts the updates you'll see on your friendfeed to those from the people whose updates and links you most commonly interact with. Other social media startups, including Path, Highlight, GroupMe, Frenzy, Rally Up, Huddl, Kik, and Shizzlr, also offer ways to limit groups to a more manageable size, a reflection of how friendships work in real life: an inner circle for true intimacy, an outer circle for all the benefits of a community at large. And when Google+ launched in 2011, many early adopters were excited about the chance to start sorting their e-friends from scratch. The new apps suggest that maybe we've

Reed
8:24 PM Nov 7

Well no more facebook friends for me. I have 285 and counting

Reed
8:25 PM Nov 7

what the heck does this word mean??????

Image 4.1 Student Comments on an Article of the Week

Mr. Hyler:	"What was one of the main reasons people like Facebook?"
Reed:	"The article said because people are too busy to keep up with their friends and their lives, and Facebook is easier."
Mr. Hyler:	"Does everyone agree with this?"
Savannah:	"Yes, but people should make time for their friends."
Mr. Hyler:	"Do you think Facebook has turned into a place where people can just see how many friends they can get?"
Emily:	"For some people, yes, and that is where they get into trouble. They could get stalked by people they don't know."

The students decode the article using the comment feature on Google Docs. I ask my students to ask questions of the article, point out vocabulary they may not understand, make comments about the article, and try to make connections to other items they may have read. In Image 4.1 Reed has asked a question and made a rather interesting comment after reading about Facebook and social media.

My seventh graders are required to have at least four to five comment bubbles when decoding the article, and my eighth graders are required to have between six and eight. Inserting comment bubbles is simple and effective. The user holds down the left mouse button and highlights the part of the document he or she wants to make a comment on, and at the top of the document there is a drop down menu titled "insert" where the user can choose comment. A comment bubble appears at the right side of the document, and the user fills in the bubble with whatever question, comment, or suggestion he or she may have. As I assess my students' work with AW, I use the comments and questions my students have written for learning opportunities upon returning their articles and written responses.

The written response that accompanies the article can be adjusted to any grade level. Kelly Gallagher keeps the written response portion open-ended for his high school students. In addition, he gives them multiple options on what they can write about. My instructions are shown in Figure 4.1.

Book Review Project

As mentioned at the beginning of the chapter, I want my students to go further into the realm of informational text. I have found book reviews are a way my students can be creative, informative, and provide explanations of books read by fellow classmates. Because I want my students to read on their own outside

How to Complete Mr. Hyler's Article of the Week

I. READ THE ARTICLE (5 points)

Read and have a conversation with the text (annotate). Ask it questions, make comments, and point out words or passages you may not know.

    A. Feel free to use symbols. For instance:
        - question marks (?) for questions you have about the reading.
        - exclamation points (!) for something you learned from the text.
        - addition signs (+) for parts of the reading you agree with.
        - subtraction signs (-) for parts of the reading you don't agree with.
    B. Demonstrate evidence of close reading. Mark any other reactions you have as you read. In addition to using symbols, you MUST include writing in the margin. This will help guide your thinking when you are completing the written response at the end.
        - 7th graders—use at least 3 symbols and 3 written reactions on each page.
        - 8th graders—use at least 5 symbols and 5 written reactions on each page.

II. WRITTEN RESPONSE (10 points)

The written response should include the following:

    A. Begin by writing a 4-5 sentence summary about the article (***paragraph #1***). Below is an example of a summary written about a short story that was read. (3 points)
        - In the short story "The Secret Life of Walter Mitty," author James Thurber presents a character that fantasizes about himself as a hero enduring challenging circumstances. In his real life, Walter Mitty lives an ordinary, plain life. He is a husband under the control of a nagging wife. Thurber uses dialogue to give readers an understanding of Mitty's character. The story takes place over a period of twenty minutes; during this brief time, Mitty drives his wife to the hairdresser and does errands that his wife has given him while he waits for her.

When writing your summary, keep these things in mind:

- Do not rewrite the original piece.
- Keep your summary short.
- Use your own wording.
- Refer to the central and main ideas of the original piece.
- Read with who, what, when, where, why and how questions in mind.

    B. Who is the audience for this article? Is it written for a general audience or for everyone? Is it a special audience? For example, did the author write this for scientist, teachers, or kids? You need to provide **specific evidence** or **support from the text**. An example of using evidence from the text is done for you below; the italicized print is the actual quote from the article that was read. (***Paragraph #2***). (2 points)
        - This article was written for scientist. In paragraph two, sentence one, it says *"the scientific community is in an uproar over the release of the parasite into the wild and thinks it could destroy important habitat"*.
    C. What is the author's reason or purpose for writing this piece? Was the author trying to inform, persuade, explain, entertain, or motivate? What specific evidence from the article supports your answer? An example has been provided for you below, the italicized print is the actual quote from the article that was read (***Paragraph #3***). (2 points)

Figure 4.1 Instructions for Article of the Week

(Continued)

Figure 4.1 (Continued)

For example: The author's purpose was to persuade the reader not to drink as much caffeine. In paragraph five it discusses how harmful it can be to children under fourteen years old and the health concerns associated with it. *"Medical research has shown an increased amount of restlessness among teens when caffeine is ingested."*

    D. What is your opinion of the article and why do you have this opinion (**Paragraph #4**)? Again, use specific evidence from the article to support your opinion. The italicized print is the actual quote from the article that was read. (3 points)

For example: In my opinion, I think the article brings up a lot of important points about use of military force in Iraq. Though I am not a violent person, the author does a great job supporting his argument for the use of force. For instance, in the last paragraph he states, *"the use of force to control such terrorist activity can potentially derail any other terrorist groups from be compelled to do the same."*

* Points will be lost due to incompletion of the assignment and incomplete parts of the assignment. In addition, points will be lost for poor conventions and sentence structure throughout the written response.

---

of school, a book review gives an insight into a book without the teacher standing in front of the class going on and on how good a book is and why. The students rely on their peers for a true book analysis.

Besides students writing a review, we spend time thinking about how they can make themselves sound credible when it comes to their written review. I break the book review project down into three parts, each worth about one third of the project's overall grade:

- Reading logs
- Written book review
- Digital book trailer or digital comic strip

I spend a total of four weeks on this project. I give the students two weeks to read their selected book, one week to complete the written book review, and one week to complete their digital book trailer or a digital comic strip. This could be adjusted. During the two weeks the students are reading, we spend considerable time looking at formal and nonformal reviews to prepare the students. Nonformal reviews are book reviews you might find on Amazon, Goodreads, or even Barnes & Noble that everyday people put on the sites. Then, I bring in newspapers and magazines that contain formal reviews so students can analyze formal reviews given to books, movies, or perhaps new products. By comparing formal and nonformal reviews side by side, students can see similarities and differences between the two. In addition to just showing models and discussing reviews, I give a formal book review as an article of the week during the project to help solidify the students' understanding of a review's intended audience and purpose.

Reading Logs

I have always struggled with the use of reading logs (Image 4.2). First, when I assign homework, I want it to be meaningful homework. Assigning homework continues to be a debate among educators today. When it comes to the reading log, I had strongly considered ruling it out. In the past when I did any type of reading project, I gave my students more of a pacing guide to help them stay on track with their reading, but never assigned a reading log. In fact, the pacing guide was not an assignment but more of a reference tool.

My biggest fear with giving a reading log is students will not only fudge the time they put on the log, but they will also forge their parent's signature. To help curve any temptation by potential forgers, I put an academic integrity clause at the bottom of the reading log. Getting middle school students to read is tough, and I don't want to discourage them further by adding a reading log. Therefore, I assign the reading log during the second half of the year and have them complete it every week. I don't want the purpose of the log, which is to encourage them to read outside of the classroom, to be lost.

Students do not earn points based on the number of pages read or minutes spent reading. Instead, each student is responsible for reading five out of the seven days during a given week for a minimum of 15 minutes. They need to record the date, title of the book, minutes spent reading, and the number of

Table 4.2 MAPS for Reading Responses

Mode	Reading reflection and personal response
Media	Google Docs
Audience(s)	Teacher
Purpose(s)	Monitor students' reading outside of the classroom and check comprehension
Situation	This is a document primarily for me, the teacher; I expect students to keep track of their thoughts while reading a formal piece of writing by providing 8 to 10 sentences, with correct grammar and spelling.

pages read. I have adjusted the time according to how much they are required to read in high school. In addition, I have my students complete a reading response with each log they turn in. They get to choose from a list of 14 sentence starters, which can be seen in Image 4.2. Students share their response with me via

Name _____

WEEKLY INDEPENDENT READING LOG
Read a minimum of 10 - 15 minutes a day, 5 days a week.

Date	Title	Pgs Read	Minutes Spent Reading

Reading Response: In a **MINIMUM OF SIX COMPLETE SENTENCES, respond specifically to one of the following prompts each week. Please make sure you have a topic sentence, detail sentences, and a wrap-up sentence. Create a new Google Document to submit your reading response.** (1) Three things I learned are... (2) A really good description is... [quote a descriptive passage] (3) The best part of this section was...because... (4) I want to know more about... (5) I can relate to [name a character] because... (6) The setting is important because... (7) This reminds me of... (8) I predict _____ will happen because... (9) These pages were boring because... (10) The theme in this story is... (11) [Name a character] surprised me when...(12) These pages were interesting because... (13) The conflict in this section is.... (14) Summarize what happened in this section.

Academic Integrity: The information above is true and accurate. I read at least 5 days this week for at least 10-15 minutes each day.

Student Signature:_____

Parent Signature:_____

Image 4.2 Reading Log Instructions

Google Drive. I typically return the responses within a few days, especially the first one because I want to eliminate any future problems the students may have with their responses.

By adding a writing component to the reading logs, it requires the students to reflect more on what they have read; this will not only help them to comprehend what they have read, but it will help them when it comes time to writing their written book review. Each reading log turned into me is worth 15 points. I give them 5 points for properly filling in the table and 10 points for their reading response.

Written Book Review

The written portion of the book review takes at least two class periods to explain to the students. The lecture portion of the written book review takes around 15 minutes. I have the lecture recorded by using an online recording tool called Audacity. Audacity, mentioned in chapter 3, is free recording software that can be downloaded on laptops or desktop computers. Audacity is user friendly, and the files created by it can be easily converted into MP3 files or WAV files so a teacher's recording can be used as a podcast or posted on YouTube.

I break the written book review into six sections or areas for the students to focus on (see Figure 4.2). Though it is important for students to express voice and have a polished piece of writing to submit for grading, I spend more time discussing the first four sections of the review. I don't want my students to get bogged down in concentrating too much on spelling, grammar, capitalization, or how they are crafting this particular piece of writing. Students compose their written review on Google Drive and share it with me when they are completed.

I have my students focus on four specific areas: plot summary, characters, compare/contrast, and evaluation. Also, I grade the students based on voice/organization and the proper use of grammar and mechanics. I offer the students more of a guideline rather than a rubric for this assignment. What is the difference? A rubric is designed to help both the teacher and the student. It is concrete and mandatory. It is a quantitative measurement and not flexible. A student either has met the criteria or they haven't, the latter resulting in a lower grade in a particular section. A guide allows the teacher to look for concepts but doesn't restrict the student's creativity or personal expression, which is important because I want to hear the student's voice come through with his or her written review.

Written Book Review—Part 2 of 3 (For Book Project)

Due: _____ , 2013

1. Plot Summary
- In 1–2 paragraphs describe the basic situation, theme(s), and a few of the main events of the plot. Use a vivid voice. Your goal is to hook the reader without giving away too much.

2. Character Analysis
- In 1–2 paragraphs the main character(s) are analyzed; external and internal characteristics are described. Reviewer makes connections between characters and discusses the internal and external problems the main character may have.

3. Compare / Contrast: connection to other work
- In 1–2 paragraphs, this text is compared or contrasted to another work such as a novel, poem, movie, etc. Shows strong insight about the connection.

4. Personal Evaluation and Evidence from the Text
- In 1–2 paragraphs, ranks the book from 1 (weakest) to 5 (strongest) stars and gives a strong explanation in one paragraph why he or she did/did not the book. Supports opinions throughout with 4 or more specific examples or quotes (evidence from the text). Other great readers will want to listen to this evaluation.

5. Author's Craft: voice, organization
- The student writes with strong voice throughout the review: the author uses grade level vocabulary and chooses interesting word choice. The review is well organized and there is the use of transitions between ideas.

6. Conventions: neatness, punctuation, capitalization, spelling, and grammar
- Includes: evidence of a consistent, strong command of all grade level conventions. No spelling, punctuation, grammar, or capitalization errors. Typed using Arial, Times New Roman, Helvetica, with font size no bigger than 12 and titles no bigger than 14.

___/25 Points

Figure 4.2 Instructions for Book Review

I give two class periods for students to work on their reviews. This time does not count time they may have worked on it outside of school. To begin, I spend the first day modeling for students how to write a quality compare/contrast paragraph. The compare/contrast section of the book review acts as a practice for the seventh graders for when we write our bigger compare/compare contrast paper after we finish our myths. Though I find value in students composing a compare/contrast paper, that paper will not be discussed in this book. Yet, later in this chapter, I will describe the myths that my students write and how we approach this task from an informational perspective.

During the second day, students are put into small groups and peer revise their reviews for improvement. Students get into groups no bigger than five so they have enough time to communicate with their peers throughout the

Image 4.3 Students Respond to One Another's Writing Using Google Docs

process. Each student takes a turn and reads his or her review out loud to the group. As the individual is reading, the other students are adding comments and questions by inserting comment bubbles on the side of the document (see Image 4.3). After the individual student is done reading, each member of the group shares his or her comments, concerns, and questions while the writer sits patiently and listens. After each group member is done commenting, the writer then has an opportunity to speak and discuss with the group what suggestions have been made. This process continues until all members of the group have had the opportunity to read and receive feedback. During this time I am also meeting with students about their reviews and discussing possible revisions or editing. The students bring their laptop to me as I work one on one with them.

Because students are composing the review on Google Drive, I do ask them to put links to author Web sites and to include an image of their book cover embedded into their review. Students need to have the understanding that most reviews that are online provide much more information than just the review itself. Readers are invited to read about the author and other works he or she may have. In addition, things such as pictures of book covers can have potential appeal to readers and draw them in to reading the book. These are all ways that writing has changed because more people are browsing the Internet for potential book titles, which is why I have my students engage in composing digital book trailers and comic strips (Table 4.3).

Video Book Trailers and Comic Strips

Along with the more formal elements of the book review project—the reading logs and actual book review—I invite my students to compose with different media. When it comes to students working on the book trailers and comic strips, the students can hardly contain their excitement. Students are anxious to play around in Toondoo and create a book trailer. The comic strips and book trailers allow those students who may not excel in written expression with more formal writing to excel in the creativity of making a comic or video while still following the guidelines that have been set before them. On the other hand, what those students don't realize is they are expressing themselves.

To begin, I show two digital book trailers to the students. If you access YouTube and search for "book trailers," you can find a vast array of them. I highly recommend that you preview any book trailers you find on YouTube. Adults or perhaps even publishing companies professionally create some trailers as a means to promote a book. With some careful research, a teacher can locate amateur examples done by students. I show my students digital book trailers on *Wonder* by R. J. Palacio (2012) and *Hold Me Closer Necromancer* by Lish McBride (2012), two books that are in my library. Yes, I am trying to send subliminal messages to my students. Sneaky, huh?

Table 4.3 MAPS for Video Book Trailers and Comic Strips

Mode	Remix existing material from the novel or recast material from the book to display it in a comic format.
Media	Create a digital video using Animoto or WeVideo. Students use video, images, graphics, narration, effects, music. Comic using ToonDoo or Pixton
Audience(s)	Teachers, peers, parents
Purpose(s)	For both teaching visual literacy and drawing elements from the students' reviews Comic: Students demonstrate understanding of the story by using: (plot points, creating a potential sequel, or using a different character's perspective of the story) Trailer: compare to movie trailers; be sure to give enough information to be make the audience interested but not so much that you give the story away
Situation	Look at three digital book trailers; note the similarities and differences

As we look at the book trailers I ask my students to think about the elements they used in their digital stories from chapter 3 such as music, text, pictures, and drawings and how these elements could add to the book trailer along with how they could hook the potential reader. We make comparisons to movie trailers and the blurb that is written on the back and inside sleeve of most books. Next, I ask the following questions:

- What did the creator do to hook the potential reader?

- How did the music enhance the overall effect of the trailer?

- What parts of the plot can be used without giving away too much of the book?

- Does the use of video instead of pictures or drawings make the trailer more appealing to the reader or does that depend on the book?

Students write down their answers in their journal, and from that point we begin the planning process for the video by completing a storyboard similar to the one discussed in chapter 3. As the teacher, you have the freedom to choose how students complete the planning process for their book trailer.

When students have completed the planning step, I let them reacquaint themselves with Animoto and WeVideo. I generally give the students four full class periods to complete the book trailer. This highly depends on the time of year, availability of the mobile laptop carts, and other impending issues that may arise.

Those students who may not want to take the route of doing a digital book trailer may want to explore the other option I give them, which is doing a comic strip. There are plenty of available tools to use for creating comic strips or what might be referred to as graphic texts. Graphic novels themselves have gained popularity. Jeff Kinney's *Diary of a Wimpy Kid* series (2011) and James Patterson's *Middle School* series, along with his latest title, *I Funny* (Patterson & Park, 2012), are very popular among elementary and middle school students alike.

With this genre gaining so much popularity, it is no wonder I get a positive response from my students when I tell them they can create a comic strip about their book. I give them a few options on what to create.

- Choose a particular scene from your book and recreate it as a comic.

- Create as a comic strip an alternate ending to your book.

- Create a comic strip using the perspective of another character in the book.
- Present a comic strip that summarizes the book you have read.

Along with creating the comic strip, the students have to provide a half-page explanation of their comic strip. This helps me to better understand what the students have composed.

There are two sites I recommend for composing a comic strip. There is Toondoo.com and Pixton.com. In the past I have always used Toondoo as my go to Web site. Lately, it seems it is slow and may provide log-in difficulties for my students. Toondoo is easy to use, and it makes it extremely simple for students to share their comic with me for grading. In addition, the log-in process is easy for students if the website is not acting slow. Pixton has a more complex sign-up process, but students like it better than Toondoo because they can manipulate the characters more within each window of their comic.

No matter what or how you have students create with the book review project, the students are being exposed to different forms of literature and learning how to inform and explain what they have learned via different venues. Please visit our companion wiki for student examples (createcomposeconnect. wikispaces.com).

Myths

Throughout this book, I am trying to show the connections that can be made between the three different genres that are the focus of the CCSS. Writing isn't just informational, argumentative, and narrative. Last year at the Michigan Reading Association Conference, I sat in on Jeff Anderson's session for his recent book *Ten Things Every Writer Needs to Know* (2011). I always know when I have been to an excellent PD session when I walk away with ample notes (and a desire to buy the speaker's book). Anderson spent the beginning of his session talking about the concept of quality writing and how that writing involves narrative, argumentative, and informational characteristics; the exact three genres that are focused on by the CCSS. In his book he discusses the idea of using fiction models when teaching nonfiction writing. He agrees it would be good to model persuasive essay examples when teaching students how to write persuasive essays. However, he argues it should not "preclude us from learning and applying elements we see in fiction across forms" (2011, p. 36). Teachers should be encouraged to use any genre or form to serve as a model for any writing task we may have our students complete. Even if this means, when teaching informational writing, using literature that is viewed more for its narrative qualities as opposed to its informational qualities. Often times I am questioned why I teach myths to my students during an informational unit, and it is Anderson's advice that guides me.

My rationale for teaching myths as informational can perhaps be better understood if teachers know that I tie in social studies aspects with each of the myths we read. I put a world map up in my room, and I put a pin at each part of the world we have visited. For instance, we start our myth unit reading Persephone and Demeter, one of many Greek myths. As we discuss background information, I place a pin in Greece on the map, and we learn about the Greek culture. We then continue on to Iraq with Mesopotamian culture, and then we journey to Egypt with The Secret Name of Ra. From there we head to India for Hindu myths.

In addition to going cross-curricular with social studies, we talk about the idea of why myths were created and why they still exist today. The purpose of myths being told was to explain the unexplainable. Earlier in the chapter I mentioned that informational writing itself is meant to inform and explain something to readers. Well, aren't myths doing just that? Indeed, I know, myths aren't factual. Think about the Bible though; do we really know if what is written is factual? Without getting into a religious debate, Christianity and the Bible help us to understand the unexplainable. Having my students look at myths through the lens of an informational text is challenging, but not overwhelmingly difficult. Myths are also designed to teach a lesson, which is a really big part of our daily conversations we have about myths. What lessons we learn from myths are put to the forefront of our discussion because the students will be writing their own myths. Furthermore, when we collaborate with another classroom outside of our district via Google Hangout, we discuss the lessons learned in each of the myths we read and why they are important. The myths listed here are ones I read and are read by the class we collaborate with.

1. Persephone and Demeter
2. Narcissus
3. The Epic of Gilgamesh
4. How Odin Lost His Eye
5. Theseus and the Minotaur
6. The Secret Name of Ra

With this book being about the CCSS language arts classroom and the implementation of the technology, it important to discuss how that technology furthers my students' learning capabilities inside of the myth unit. There are two ways I implement technology into our myth unit. I use Google Hangouts, which is available through Google's social media platform, Google Plus.

Using a tool such as Google Hangout does not require every student to log into his or her Google account; also, because Google Plus and Google Hangout are considered social media, a teacher may need to gain permission from the tech director or administrator. Google Hangout is where you can video chat face to face. A teacher can create a hangout or get invited to one. Skype is another potential option, but it does not offer tools such as document collaboration or screen sharing.

Aram Kabodian, a writing project colleague and fellow middle school teacher at MacDonald Middle School in East Lansing, Michigan, during a writing group session we were both a part of earlier this year, hatched the idea of our classes collaborating. We both teach seventh graders and discovered we both teach myths. What I find interesting is the idea to get our classrooms to chat with one another came from meeting on Google Hangout. It was easy to say we wanted to get our classes together and have the students chat, but we needed a plan. We couldn't just have our classrooms meet in a virtual space and say, "Chat!"

Before discussing the plan that Kabodian and I had, I want to elaborate on the why. To some professionals it might look like just another excuse to infuse technology into the classroom. However, this is not the case. Besides curricular reasons for collaboration, we deemed it necessary to talk to our students about how collaboration works outside of school. Collaboration is vital to many jobs. Kabodian and I deem it important to show examples where writing and collaboration are important.

In addition to the collaboration piece, we felt it was important to get our students to step outside the bubbles I mentioned earlier. The school where I teach has around 120 students, most of whom are white. Kabodian's school has a vast array of cultures represented, and there are just over 700 students present. We deemed it appropriate to introduce our students to each other to show the varying cultural differences. My students especially need to be exposed to different cultures, seeing how they are part of a community that is predominantly white and rural, with only a few students of color attending our school.

Finally, Kabodian and I wanted our classrooms to discuss the myths we were reading in our classrooms, especially since I take the approach that myths offer information, and Kabodian addresses them in more of a narrative sense. As teachers we deem it important for students to see the different perspectives that people can have on literature. In addition, we felt it would be beneficial for students to discuss the lessons that are presented in myths and discuss how these lessons can be applied in today's world and within our students' different cultural beliefs.

It is our professional judgment that technology can truly enhance an experience for students. The idea of two classes reaching out to connect about a common curriculum can show students they are not alone when it comes to what is being taught by their teachers. In addition, we as teachers can learn from each other. For example, Kabodian and I have learned a cornucopia of instructional strategies and tools, which each of us is implementing into our own classroom. Not only are our students learning, but we also are learning from each other as well and making each other better educators.

To get our students on the path to being better-rounded learners, we do a 20-minute "hangout" to introduce our students to each other. Each of us has a set of questions prepared in advance for our students to ask of each other. I simply choose some volunteers to step in front of the camera and ask the questions. Each of our classes had completed a "This I Believe" essay. This was talked about in chapter 3. We use the essay as a way for our students to get to know each other, using an online site called Youth Voices (youthvoices.net).

Youth Voices is a school-based social network that was started in 2003 by a group of National Writing Project teachers. We merged several earlier blogging projects. We have found that there are many advantages to bringing students together in one site that lives beyond any particular class. It's easier for individual students to read and write about their own passions, to connect with other students, comment on each other's work, and create multimedia posts for each other.

More information is available at youthvoices.net/about and on the National Writing Project's Digital Is Web site (digitalis.nwp.org) under the resource titled "Authentic Conversations on Youth Voices." See the blog posts in Image 4.4.

The students post their essays on Youth Voices under a discussion I have started. Even though there are about the same number of students in each of the classes, Kabodian and I direct each of our students to respond to at least two specific students with the freedom to respond to more than just those two who have been assigned. By the students doing this, they begin the necessary dialogue needed so they can get comfortable when we have more Google Hangouts and post more pieces of writing on Youth Voices—for example, the myths the students will be working on.

Image 4.4 Student Blog Post on Youth Voices

Prior to my students posting their essays on Youth Voices, I have them go back and reflect on the essays they wrote. My students wrote theirs back in late September, and I want them to look back on their writing and see if their beliefs might have changed or to make deeper revisions such as where they might add more detail or what parts they can potentially remove. In addition, we discuss how the essays might change because a different audience will be reading them. It is no longer just their teacher, their parents/guardians, or even their fellow classmates. They are now putting themselves out there for the rest of the world to see. I explain to my students, when they publish their writing, they open themselves up to more constructive criticism and feedback. To me, this will truly help the students become better writers.

As the students are becoming better writers, Kabodian and I arrange to do more Google Hangouts, and our students dive deeper into myths. We have our classes discuss the following questions:

- What myths are each of our classes are reading?
- What lessons did we learn or take away from our myths?
- How can we apply these lessons to our lives today?

- What have we learned about the cultures the myths originated in?

- What myths do we have today, and how do they help explain our own culture or cultures?

- What are some potential topics we could choose to write our own myth on?

These questions can lead to some in-depth conversations that may require more than one or two Google Hangouts. In the end, each class composes its own myths from the ideas that have been generated. Below are a few questions for students to discuss and consider.

- Why is the sky blue?

- Why do the moon, the earth, and sun rotate as they do?

- Why does the moon glow?

- Why do people die?

- How do we make cheese?

- Why are evergreen trees always green?

- Why can't humans breathe underwater?

- Why are the stars so far away?

- Why can't we fly?

- Why do we go to school?

How students write their myths is completely up to the teacher. Kabodian and I each have different approaches. In the end, our students will post their myths on Youth Voices and, again, will receive feedback from each other on the Web site. After the feedback, my students reflect on the comments left by the other class, and I have the students write in their journals about the overall experience of publishing their writing online—not only the importance of collaborating with another class but also how it made them a more well-rounded writer. Overall, the students really enjoy the experience and even bring up the idea of using Google Hangout as a tool to help them with homework. As their teacher, I am pleased with their thoughts and comments.

What's Next?

Informational writing will continue to be at the forefront of our teaching in the language arts classroom. The CCSS pushes for nonfiction reading and writing, and when we look at how we are going to make the effort to incorporate this into our classroom, collaboration with our own colleagues is crucial to the success of our students. As long as we look to do more writing across the curriculum, implementing more nonfiction such as the informational writing discussed in this chapter will not take extended amounts of time like some educators think. Even our gym teacher requires middle school students to turn in an article every two weeks about something that is trending in physical education. The students in the middle school work on summarization of the articles they find and nothing more, but at least they are practicing writing skills in an arena other than the language arts classroom.

Of course, informational writing is only part of the equation. There is emphasis on argumentative writing as well with the CCSS. Argumentative writing is another skill that will propel our students to be more successful in the college arena as well as the work force. Middle school teachers as well as high school teachers will need to put emphasis on argumentative writing. In the next chapter, we will not only discuss specific lessons and activities for argumentative writing but also talk about the differences between being persuasive and being argumentative.

5 | Looking for Evidence (Argumentative)

Expressing our opinions could be considered *the* fundamental element of our democracy. We watch protesters make impassioned pleas, we listen to politicians debate major issues, and we discuss our own thoughts and feelings over coffee and, more recently, through social networks.

Yet, with all of this discussion going on, where do our students get a chance to see genuine disagreements and compromises discussed with clear, logical arguments? In all of the chatter and hype, where do our students learn how to create an effective, well-reasoned argument, the kind that can lead to genuine dialogue and perhaps even compromise? Certainly not on the hundreds of hours of TV and radio shows produced each day, nor on the Web forums of many major news sites or blogs. There are enough disagreements in one day's worth of news media to keep us all fighting for many more days, weeks, months, and years.

Yet, one thing that we can all agree on is this: writing and thinking are intertwined skills. And, if we want our students to be smart, critical thinkers, then we need to make sure they are also need to be clear, logical writers. As a teacher of writing, I feel this way not just because writing is in the CCSS but also because my students come to school with many opinions, often the opinions of other people in their lives, and I want them to develop their own lines of thinking.

More importantly, differentiating between fact and opinion is not a skill that I can teach in just one day, checking it off the list. In this global society, students will have to understand how to differentiate between facts and opinions as well as various interpretations of facts. What they see on TV, hear on the radio, and read on the Internet are often one small slice of an entire story and usually backed up with more opinions than logical reasoning.

W.8.1—Write arguments to support claims with clear reasons and relevant evidence.

a. Introduce claim(s), acknowledge and distinguish the claim(s) from alternate or opposing claims, and organize the reasons and evidence logically.
b. Support claim(s) with logical reasoning and relevant evidence, using accurate, credible sources and demonstrating an understanding of the topic or text.
c. Use words, phrases, and clauses to create cohesion and clarify the relationships among claim(s), counterclaims, reasons, and evidence.
d. Establish and maintain a formal style.
e. Provide a concluding statement or section that follows from and supports the argument presented.

So, this all leads me (and many of the teachers I work with) to what seems to be a simple question: What is the difference between persuasion and argument? As I have talked with my colleagues and students regarding what makes a good argument, we all agree that there has been a paradigm shift from our previous views on persuasion. Simply using techniques—such as a bandwagon appeal, an endorsement or testimonial, or the final call to action—to attract a reader to one side of an issue is no longer sufficient for our students. They can (and *should*) understand persuasion, yet they also need to know the techniques of effective argumentation. The CCSS calls for it. Literacy leaders call for it. And our kids deserve it.

Before sharing examples of how my seventh and eighth graders learn how to use arguments effectively, I want to delve a little deeper into that seemingly simple question of how students use arguments effectively so I can make the case for argument writing in my classroom.

Elements of Argument

Teaching argument is nothing new for those of us interested in writing; Aristotle described the different types of rhetorical appeals centuries ago. What's different now, with the advent of the CCSS and our improved attention to modeling and scaffolding writing instruction, is that teachers and students have the opportunity to really take arguments apart and look at them carefully, and then construct their own arguments based on high-quality mentor texts. As I think about how to teach argument to my students, I recognize three pieces of this puzzle that I need to examine with them: the language of argument, the moves that writers make in arguments, and the differences between argumentation and persuasion.

The Language of Argument

First, there are a few terms about argument writing addressed in the CCSS that could use a little elaboration. Also, some of our most trusted colleagues who study the teaching of writing have a few more ideas to add based on the Toulmin model for argumentation, and we will bring in their voices, too. The first three terms come in the overarching standard CCSS.ELA-Literacy.W.8.1: "Write arguments to support claims with clear reasons and relevant evidence."

> **Claim**—the assertion, the case that the writer is trying to make. In school, English teachers have typically called this the "thesis." However, a claim must be "debatable and defensible" (Smith, Wilhelm, & Fredricksen, 2012, p. 13). In other words, a claim is an invitation into an intellectual conversation, not simply a statement of "the way it is."
> **Evidence**—the data, or what Stephen Toulmin calls the "grounds" for a claim. One of the phrases that we hear often is "details and examples," but evidence is more than that. Different types of evidence matters depending on the argument you want to make. For instance, a first person retelling may count as evidence in a historical documentary about a crime, but DNA and bullet casings would be necessary evidence to make a forensic analysis.
> **Reasons**—the basis or justification for a certain type of evidence. As noted above, a particular kind of evidence counts in different contexts, and writers need to justify how the evidence they are using supports the claim they are making. This is where the reasons come into play. Smith and colleagues and Hillocks (2011) refer to Toulmin's use of the term *warrant* as the backing for particular kinds of evidence, and Smith and colleagues even call warrants "the heart of the argument" (2012, p. 15).

The fourth term comes from one of the substandards, CCSS.ELA-Literacy. W.8.1a: "Introduce claim(s), acknowledge and distinguish the claim(s) from alternate or opposing claims, and organize the reasons and evidence logically."

Alternate or Opposing Claims (Counterargument)—This element of the argument demonstrates the writer's ability to see all sides, acknowledging and heading off the argument of an opponent. Smith and colleagues (2012) add in "rebuttals," "qualifiers," and "responses" to this category as well, showing that the writer may have to take some time to defend against these alternative positions.

The Moves That Writers Make in Arguments

I am really beginning to explore the idea of how to help my students think like expert writers. Over the past few years, I have heard about the idea of using what Graff, Birkenstein, and Durst call "templates" (2011) or what Fisher and Frey call "sentence frames" (2011). No matter what you call these tools, the idea is simple: we need to teach our students how to make the connections between ideas in their academic writing. Academic and professional writing relies on clear transitions that show the relationships between different ideas that are either alike or different, parallel to one another, or totally opposite. For instance, Fisher and Frey offer a few sentence frames as elements that students can use in their writing:

- The evidence shows that _____
- I believe this because _____
- Ultimately, what I believe is _____
- I reached this conclusion because _____
- I would even add that _____ (2011, p. 66)

There is a useful video on the Teaching Channel about how to use sentence frames, as well as documents with dozens of frames on the Best Practices for ELLs Web site (both linked from the chapter 5 page in the wiki). Sometimes, even having a list of appropriate transitional words and phrases is enough to get students moving in the right direction. The Purdue Online Writing Lab (OWL) offers this list of transitional words and phrases, which also is available as a link from the wiki page.

By using these types of templates or frames, I can help my students think about the relationships between different facts and examples, drawing connections or making a contrast between the broader ideas they are writing about. This is much different than simply trying to persuade people (or, for that matter, to coax, prompt, or sway them). Instead, learning how to argue is one piece of learning how to think critically, listen to others, and make a strong case for what you believe to be the best course of action. Observe the two different paragraphs lifted from two 8th grade students' (Kristen and Teagan) police report writing modeled after Hillock's book; it demonstrates their use of these frames.

> **The evidence does show and support** what the witness has reported. First of all, since the killer had his right hand on the wall then his feet would be pointed to the left and footprint X are facing to the left and go in the right direction. Also, person C's silverware are on the left side so that means he is left handed and the shooter is left handed. Person A's chair is point blank range so this is even more evidence.
>
> This evidence leads me to believe that Person C is guilty. **I reached this conclusion because** person C is left handed due to his silverware on the left side of his plate. Also, the killer had his right hand on the wall so that means he had to shoot with his left hand so all this evidence is pointing toward person C. (Hillocks, 2011)

The Differences between Argumentation and Persuasion

A final component of this conversation comes from how Hillocks and Smith and colleagues deal with the differences between persuasion and argument. In short, they don't. Hillocks devotes only one paragraph to the idea (2011, p. 17) and Smith and colleagues state, "We don't think the distinction between argument and persuasion is especially useful, so we won't be making that distinction" (2012, p. 17). Troy and I respectfully disagree. In the conversations that we have had with other teachers, the differences between argument and persuasion are at the heart of how we teach this kind of writing.

One helpful resource that I have found outlines some of the differences between argument and persuasion. What I like about the T-chart from Smekens Education Solutions (2012; also linked on our wiki) is that it does make clear the difference between one-sided, "winner take all" persuasive writing as compared to the two-sided (or more), thoughtful conversation that takes place in argument writing. In looking at that chart, there are some points I don't agree with. For instance, it says that a writer of an argument "doesn't need an audience to

Table 5.1 Traits of *Argumentation* and *Persuasion*

• Actions in Argumentation
  ○ Reason
  ○ Support
  ○ Interpret
• Features
  ○ Facts and data (both sides)
  ○ Acknowledgement of other side
  ○ Grapples with the issues
• Tone
  ○ Balanced
  ○ Debate and refutation
  ○ Agreement and disagreement
  ○ Takes a defensible stance
• Uses the "PAWS" Approach
  ○ Position (claim)
  ○ Acknowledge
  ○ Warrant (rationale)
  ○ Support (data and evidence)
	• Actions in Persuasion
	  ○ Appeal
	  ○ Influence
	  ○ Spin/advertise
	• Features
	  ○ Own opinion
	  ○ Limited facts and data
	  ○ Elements of propaganda
	• Tone
	  ○ Aggressive
	  ○ One-sided
	  ○ Emotional
	  ○ Potential lack of credibility
	• Uses the "LOCK" Approach
	  ○ Loaded words
	  ○ Overstatements
	  ○ Carefully chosen facts
	  ○ Key omissions

convince" (Smekens Education Solutions, 2012). Of course the writer needs an audience to convince; he or she just doesn't have to be so heavy handed about it when presenting an argument as compared to a purely persuasive piece.

So, where does this leave me when I think about how to get my students to understand the difference between argument and persuasion? I'm not sure that I have all the answers yet, but one resource that Troy developed with some social studies teachers in a Teaching American History project in the summer of 2012 might help (see Table 5.1). During that workshop, they built off the T-chart idea and listed some vocabulary that would help differentiate argumentation and persuasion. It's not an exhaustive list, yet Troy and I hope that it provides some concrete examples for how to talk with your students about the differences between argument and persuasion.

Making Connections

Yelling. Firm. Loud. Strict. Fierce. These are the terms spit out by my seventh graders when I ask them to tell me what their definition of an argument is. However, not all of my students feel there needs to be yelling or loud voices. My students do understand that an argument can take place between two people or two sides, and they do understand it is a matter of opinion. For example, a student from my first hour class stated in her journal:

My definition of an argument is when two or more people have different opinions and want to prove that their opinion is right.

The student is not far off from having a complete understanding of the term *argument*. When I extend the question further into having the students define what argument writing is, the findings become even more interesting.

An argumentative writing is a writing that you support only the side of the story that you believe. Also, you are supposed to persuade the reader to join your side of the conflict.

While the student has a very well thought out response, there is an obvious misunderstanding about the difference between being persuasive and argumentative. So, my seventh graders and I create a Google Document that has a two-sided table or a table with two columns, where the students and I discuss the differences between being persuasive and being argumentative (available on the companion site: createcomposeconnect.wikispaces.com). Though the table may not get as full as the one created by teachers and presented earlier in the chapter (Table 5.1), the students and I were able to display a few definitive differences so the students can be more successful when it comes to writing in the world of argument.

First, I want my students to think about times when they have tried to persuade their parents or guardians to do something or go somewhere. Second, I mention to them what Darth Vader says to Luke Skywalker about coming to the dark side. I joke with them that persuasion is very similar to Darth Vader's attempt to lure Luke to be part of the empire. Between the two examples, they get a chuckle because at least they can recall the numerous times they have tried to persuade their parents to go somewhere or do something, and this proves to be enough to getting my point across.

In order to help my students understand argument, then, we tackle, in seventh grade, public service announcements and, in eighth, police reports.

Public Service Announcements

The project itself can take anywhere from two to three weeks, depending on availability to technology and the amount of class time committed to working on the project. To begin this project, as a class, we discuss what exactly public service announcements are and why they are on television and the radio.

Table 5.2 MAPS for Public Service Announcements

Mode	Argumentative
Media	Radio broadcasts, slideshows, videos produced with portable cameras or smartphones
Audience	Teacher, classmates, other adults and students
Purpose	To start the process of students learning about making a claim in an argument and supporting that claim with facts and statistics
Situation	Students complete outlines and storyboards for their PSA projects and then move into production. From there, the PSAs are published in an online space for others to view.

I direct my students' attention to the Sarah McLachlan animal cruelty commercial (available on YouTube and as a link on our wiki). In my opinion the most important questions to ask the students about the public service announcement (PSA) are the following:

- What message is the PSA trying to get across?
- What emotion is the PSA trying to evoke?
- What position has been taken in the PSA, or what is it claiming about the topic?

By asking these questions, the students are beginning to understand not only how a PSA is structured but also the idea of forming an argument. As we discuss these questions, I use the vocabulary *claim*, *evidence*, and *reasons*. For instance, when a student answers any of the above questions, I follow up with asking him or her what *evidence* from the public service announcement can be used to support his or her answer.

While the vocabulary is very important to use with the students, at this point I want my students to be thinking about topics that are controversial and ones they could possibly choose for the PSA project. The students explore different topics by collaborating on a Google Doc. I share a public link with the students through Schoology, and the students write down a list of topics on the Google Doc (Image 5.1).

One of the things I noticed as the students were composing their list is that they were including issues they had read about in their articles of the week. For example, they listed caffeine, the postal service, and school shootings in

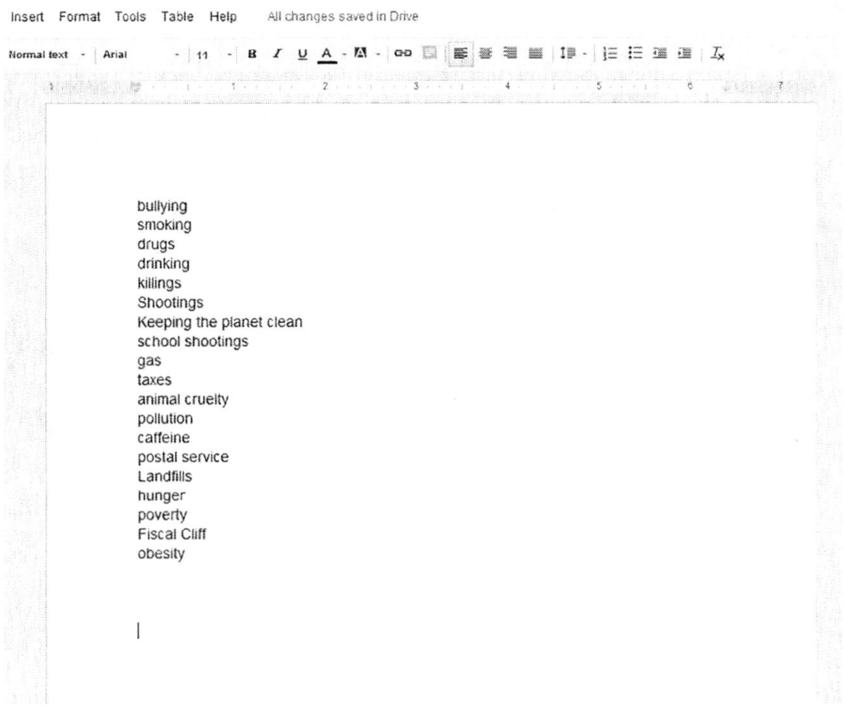

Insert   Format   Tools   Table   Help   All changes saved in Drive

Normal text   -   Arial   -   11   -   B   I   U   A   -   A   -   ∞   □   ■   ■   ■   ■ |≡   - |≡   ≡   ≡   ≡ | Iₓ

bullying
smoking
drugs
drinking
killings
Shootings
Keeping the planet clean
school shootings
gas
taxes
animal cruelty
pollution
caffeine
postal service
Landfills
hunger
poverty
Fiscal Cliff
obesity

Image 5.1 Brainstorming PSA Topics in Google Docs

their list. It made me feel good that the students were referring to what they had read in the articles and looking into the topics further for their PSA project.

> W.7.9—Draw evidence from literary or informational texts to support analysis, reflection, and research.
>
> Apply *grade 7 Reading standards* to literary nonfiction (e.g., "Trace and evaluate the argument and specific claims in a text, assessing whether the reasoning is sound and the evidence is relevant and sufficient to support the claims").

From here, I put the students into groups of three. I prefer the students to complete the project in groups because not only is this the first time they have done a project of this magnitude, but also this is my first year teaching it, and I want to be able to reflect back on the project and think about what worked and what did not work with the PSA project.

Now, with the students in their groups, they begin their PSA by choosing one of the topics they collaborated on the day before and deciding if they want to create a video or an audio recording. Furthermore, students need to think about if they want to create a live video recording or a slideshow with audio embedded. Groups then need to think about what type of emotion they want to invoke. I also ask the students to think about the main idea behind their PSA. In other words, what do the students want their audience to walk away with after they listen or watch the PSA? Besides informing the audience of an issue, are they trying to just raise awareness or money? Do they want their audience to take action on the issue? When students think about the main idea, it helps them to start thinking about the next step, which is gathering information for their PSA—for instance, facts and statistics about the particular topic.

When my students are gathering information about their topic, whether it is for a PSA project or a research project, I want them to collect their data in one place. At one time I had my students write everything down on notecards, and I would require them to turn in a minimum number of cards depending on what they were working on. I really got tired of students not turning in cards because they lost them. Students who struggle with handwriting struggled with not only neatness on their note cards, but they also would run out of room on one note card and have to put information on a second or even a third. It became a pain to keep things in order, even if the cards were numbered. Hands down, it wasn't helping them stayed organized, and I found it irritating to take home a bag full of notecards.

Goodbye notecards! I no longer have my students turn them in. Instead my students use Evernote, a tool that allows you to create notes and capture pictures, Web addresses, and audio notes (Image 5.2). Evernote can be accessed across multiple devices. Furthermore, the notes can have tags placed on them to help keep them organized. However, the greatest feature is the notes can be shared with others, which works well for the PSA projects where there are multiple students collaborating. Oh, and it is free, but the user has the option to upgrade for a fee.

Once students have finished gathering resources, I ask them to put together a storyboard similar to what I had them do with the digital stories mentioned in chapter 3. Yes, I even have the students who are doing a radio broadcast complete a storyboard, though theirs is more or less a script that helps guide them.

As student groups get their storyboards approved by me, they start moving into the production of their PSA. It takes the students about a week to create their final product, including editing and revising, and because most students are producing a live video recording, we use digital flip cameras. Digital flip cameras are small and portable. The flip cameras offer the students another piece of technology that isn't a laptop, cell phone, or Web site. Image 5.3 shows one of my students using his flip camera.

I do allow students to use their cell phones and iPods. Most students know their device's capabilities and feel comfortable using, say, their smartphone

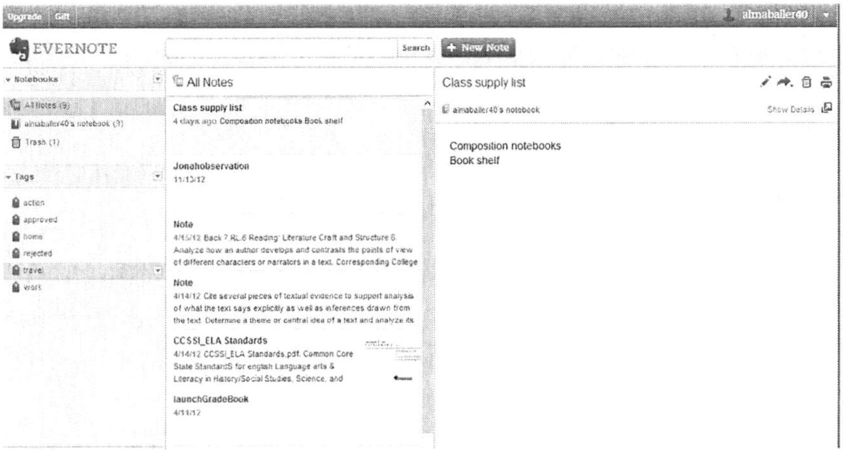

Image 5.2 Evernote

Image 5.3 Student Recording Himself with a Flip Video Camera

instead of one of the cameras. Smartphones, in particular, are an excellent resource for teachers to take advantage of when it comes to students bringing their own devices to the classroom. Smartphones have video recording capabilities that allow students to record themselves and share it with others via e-mail. If students do not want to use their own devices for voice recording, there are free sites available. I prefer to use Audacity, which is discussed in chapters 3 and 6.

PSA Wrap-Up

By having the students create videos and radio broadcasts using digital tools such as flip cams, students are inevitably practicing editing, just in a different mode. In addition, when it comes to thinking about argument writing, they are not only taking a position, but they are making a claim about a topic and understanding the reasons behind why certain music is chosen for a given commercial or the reasons why certain images are used. Also, students learn timing when they use digital tools such as Wevideo or Camtasia by having to place pictures, videos, music, and words together. Image 5.4 shows a screenshot of a PSA project about bullying and demonstrates the use of stats. Also, students learn about transitioning from one slide to the next in their video. Radio broadcasts offer yet another mode for the students to explore, and they learn to understand there is a planning process behind the creation of radio broadcasts. Professionals just don't get on the radio and start talking.

After the students hand in their public service announcements, I can usually get them returned to my seventh graders in a week. On the day we discuss project grades, I don't stand in front of the students and give them the positives and negatives. Instead, the students get out their journals, and I have them reflect back on their project to think about how they might have done it differently. Students need to do the following:

- Write down the positives and negatives they saw with the project.
- Write one to two sentences about their group and how well they collaborated.
- Answer the question, What would you have done differently if you had a chance to change any part of your project?

After they are given 10 minutes to respond, I instruct them to find a quiet spot with their PSA project group members to share their reflections. I feel it is important for students to hear if their fellow group members were critical of them

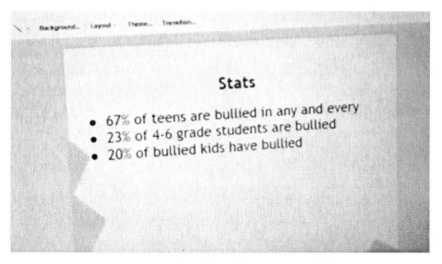

Image 5.4 Screenshot of a Student's PSA in Draft Form

or not. If they don't start hearing critical yet constructive feedback from others (especially their peers), they are going to assume they are always doing things correctly and never see any room for improvements; learning to continually seek to improve work is a lesson that can go beyond the boundaries of school walls.

Police Reports

My first year that I had to actually teach the genre of argument writing was 2011–2012. Because we were in the process of implementing the CCSS at that time, I only taught argument writing to eighth graders. As of this year (2012–2013), I now teach it to both grades. Needless to say, I was very nervous last year because I had never taught argument writing to any students. I couldn't even remember the last time I even wrote an argument essay myself. I needed some help. George Hillocks Jr. and his book *Teaching Argument Writing, Grades 6–12: Supporting Claims with Relevant Evidence and Clear Reasoning* (2011) is an excellent resource and gave me the confidence that I needed to proceed. I felt his idea to introduce students to argument writing by solving mysteries was an excellent way to get things off the ground, and it worked! I began by using a document camera, and I put a mystery picture into view for students. For example, I once used a mystery picture called "Paper Dolls," which comes from *Crime and Puzzlement 3: 24 Solve Them Yourself*

Table 5.3 MAPS for Police Reports

Mode	Argumentative
Media	Mind maps, Google Docs
Audience	Teacher, classmates
Purpose	Students write police reports to help them move into more formal writing for argument and away from PSAs.
Situation	Students will study a crime scene and develop a mind map displaying evidence they have collected, claims they are making, and the conclusions they have drawn. After completing the map, they transition into writing the report.

Picture Mysteries by Lawrence Treat and Paul Karasik (2003) (see the picture at http://tinyurl.com/ksgsj54). I like how Hillocks uses this book in his own classroom, and I have adapted it for my own classroom. This particular book is a great example for using visual literacies in the classroom, which is discussed more in chapter 7. In addition, each crime scene comes with a set of written clues to help solve the crime, in turn requiring the students to think critically about each situation that is presented.

Because they will be looking at a crime scene, I tell them they are all now rookie detectives, and we are going to work together to solve the case, in much the same way that Hillocks describes in his book. Below is a conversation I had with my 8th graders:

> "Why do we need to solve a murder?" asked Kristen.
>
> "We all need to be better argument writers and besides seeing argument writing on a test like the ACT, we need to learn how to argue more efficiently and effectively. Also, if you remember, argument is not about yelling and screaming." I replied to her.
>
> "I argue a lot with my grandpa and my mom, does that count?" jumped in Hunter.
>
> "It does to some extent Hunter, but how often do you feel your argument is heard and understood?" I responded.
>
> "Never!" Hunter shouted.
>
> "Do you want to be heard and understood, perhaps even help others see your point of view?" I ended.

Upon me asking the last question, a lot of students nod their heads yes and continue focusing on the picture I have put up on the document camera.

As mentioned earlier, my students perceive an argument as a fight, a disagreement. They think of raised voices and probably a certain type of language being used, too. This is the popular connotation of argument in our country, yet this is not what we mean when we talk about writing an argument. It takes time and practice for students to write effective arguments.

With eighth graders, I discuss that defense attorneys spend a lot of their time arguing for their client's innocence, while the prosecuting attorneys argue for a person's guilt (enter *Law & Order* music here). Though I don't want my students to get wrapped up in the whole legal system itself, I want them to focus on the main argument terms Hillocks highlights (mentioned at the beginning of the chapter), which are actually terms from Toulmin's *The Use of Argument* (2003), as I noted above. Image 5.5 is a visual representation of Toulmin's theory, which can be found in Hillocks's book.

Evidence, claim, warrant, and *rebuttals* (counterclaims) are key terms that are consistent throughout middle school and in our high school. By all of us using these terms in the middle school and high school, we are being consistent with our vocabulary; thus, students gain a better understanding of each term and how it is supposed to be used in argument writing.

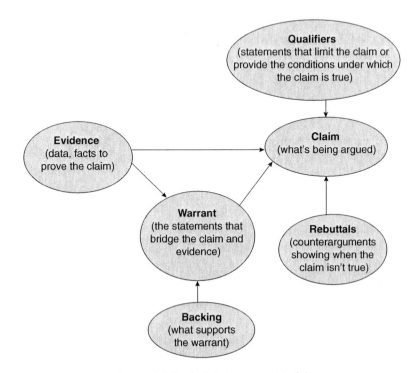

Image 5.5 Toulmin's Argument Model

Table 5.4 Helping My Students Understand Argument

What's easier for my students to understand	What's more difficult for my students to understand
Easy to gather evidence	Difficult to make a substantial claim about that evidence
Easy to look at the other side or possibilities	Difficult to express why the other side is wrong or less credible
Easy to feel impassioned about picking a side	Difficult to put their feelings aside and look at all the evidence

I try to keep in mind that the students are not producing a PSA like they did when they were in seventh grade. In eighth grade they are moving into a more formal written piece that is still using the skills they learned from their PSAs. Table 5.4 should help in understanding what I feel are the more difficult concepts middle school students face when it comes to writing argument.

At this point, we discuss the term *evidence*. On the other half of my computer I have dictionary.com pulled up with the definition of *evidence*:

Evidence—that which tends to prove or disprove something; ground for belief; proof.

I ask my students to put that definition into terms they will understand. The best response, and the most amusing, was "proof that we did something wrong—guilty." I asked the student if he had a guilty conscience and he just laughed.

I then proceed by giving the prior knowledge of the crime scene before the students are allowed to begin looking for specific evidence. When I give students the background information, I have to keep them really focused on not forming an opinion right away. Last year, students would listen to the background information and would shout out, "Guilty!" I constantly had to redirect them back to the task of gathering evidence and not being too quick to point the finger.

From here, I ask the students to find evidence in the picture that can help them create a claim about the crime. While we do this as guided practice as a whole class, I share with them a Google Document where they can write down what they see.

- chair is tipped over
- body is laying in the other room

- trash can is tipped over
- paper is out of place on the dresser
- more than one pair of scissors
- paper dolls have been made
- drink is spilled

Once I clean up the document, we go over the list again to make sure we don't need to add or remove anything. I then ask the students if they think they have enough evidence to make any type of claim.

Claim—to assert or maintain as a fact.

Moving from just finding evidence to making a claim based on that evidence is rather difficult for my students. For example, last year when my students were given a different picture, they pointed out the silverware on the counter was on the left side of the plate. However, they could not make the claim the person sitting in the chair at the counter must have been left handed, which could connect the suspect to the crime because that person was left handed. Making a claim is an area I feel students need extra practice with, and it is something that cannot be done in just a few class periods.

Though making a claim can be challenging for students, learning the reason why or exploring the reasoning behind their claim can help them to better understand the idea of argument writing. Though this is called *warrant* by other professionals, I feel middle school students better understand the term *reason*.

Reason—a basis or cause, as for some belief, action, fact, event, or other.

Though I sometimes refer to the word *warrant*, I feel that students get too tangled up in the legal implications the word has with it, so I stick with reason. While it shows great connection with the police reports the students are writing, I want them to extend the term past solving mysteries or writing such reports.

As we start to talk about bringing in the reason for their claim, I want students to start understanding the connections that are being made. I feel it is best to do this by showing my students a Web-based mind-mapping tool called Mindmeister. Mindmeister's free edition limits you to only having three maps, but students can delete one and then add another if needed. I particularly gravitate toward this tool for several different reasons.

- You can share and collaborate on the map in a way similar to Google Docs.
- Other users can edit it.
- Student can use pictures, which can be helpful to visual learners.
- Students can do a presentation with their created maps.
- Students can organize and reorganize ideas within the map.
- Students can show how ideas tie back to other ideas within the map.

For this particular assignment, the collaboration aspect is an important feature because the students write their first report together as a group. I have one student create an account and share it with others in their group. The other individuals do not need an account to access or edit the map. Second, because the eighth graders are beginning the formal process of writing an argument, students and teachers can benefit from the feature where students can tie ideas together. For example, in Image 5.6 you can see how the students tied their reasoning/concluding statement back to their evidence with a green arrow (shown here as a dotted arrow). Furthermore, after they were done analyzing all of their evidence, they decided that person X was their suspect and tied all of the information they

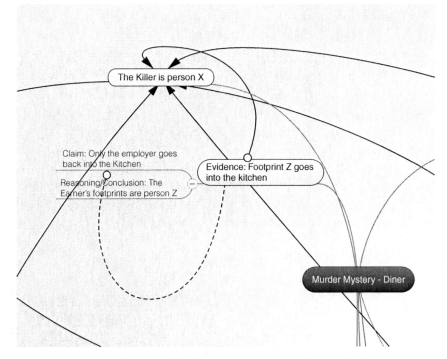

Image 5.6 Sample of Students' Brainstorming with MindMeister

had gathered to that suspect with red arrows (shown here as solid arrows). You can access the whole mind map on our wiki companion page for the book.

When it's time for students to write the formal report, they can refer to their map and see the flow of their ideas. Also, as a teacher, I can see what the thinking was by the groups/individuals and easily help them out if I see any misdirection in their thinking prior to them writing a report. I feel it is the perfect tool for teaching argument writing, and it helps students better understand Toulmin's flow chart in Image 5.5 and cuts down on time the students spend trying to figure out how to write their report. There are many other Web sites and apps where you can create mind maps to help students organize their thoughts. As with many tools, some are free with limited usage and others have cost. We've shared links to some of them on our wiki page.

When the 8th graders complete the mind map, I have them move into writing their police report. With all of the work the students have put into their mind maps, putting together their report should feel fairly painless to them, though you will always have your middle school students who complain. I make the report fairly simple for them to complete. My rubric is shown in Figure 5.1.

The group reports are done on Google Docs where the students can collaborate and share in the responsibility of completing the report. All in all, the students do a solid job of not only moving from their mind map to the report, but they produce a quality piece of formal argumentative writing (Image 5.7). I feel as their teacher, the workload is distributed equally and, if an individual student struggles with their responsibility, other group members are willing to help out and contribute. Below are a few student comments about the assignment.

Police Report

Paragraph #1—Describe in 8–10 sentences (minimum) the scene of the crime. (5 pts)

Paragraph #2—Discuss the evidence you collected from the scene of the crime in 10–12 sentences (minimum). (5 pts)

Paragraph #3—Does the evidence support what the witness has described? Explain. 4–6 sentences (minimum). (5 pts)

Paragraph #4—What conclusion can you draw from the evidence and give the reasons for your conclusion, 4–6 sentences (minimum). (5 pts)

* Please edit for sentence structure, spelling, and grammar. (5 pts)

* I do suggest breaking the report into four different sections to ensure equal participation from group members.

___/25 pts

Figure 5.1 Rubric for Police Report

"The murder scene was cool and I like how we did our brainstorming. I felt everyone did their job when we worked on the report. No one felt overwhelmed."

—Teagan

"I liked using Google Docs for the report. It was hard sometimes to concentrate when everyone was typing at the same time. Nobody complained about workload."

—Kirsten

Police Report

When we first arrived on the scene, there was a man lying face down with his right hand under his head. He still had his hat on. There are also footprints and some are leading to the kitchen. The special of the day is pea soup for $1.65. The cash register is wide open and there is cash hanging out. Person A's food has not been touched and the check is next to his plate of food. The murderer's hand print on the wall is his right hand so he shot with his left hand. Person B, C, and D's food is all gone. There is water all over the floor and there's an empty bucket with a mop by the murderer's hand print. The water stops just a few feet from the dead man lying on the floor.

There is a lot of evidence in this case. One piece of evidence is the handprint on the wall. The handprint belongs to the murder. It's a right hand print so this mean if you have your right hand on the wall, that you had to have shot with your left hand. So after looking at it, the murder must have shot with his left hand. Another piece of evidence is person C's silverware is on the left side. If your silverware is on the left side, you will more than likely eat with your left hand. So person C is left handed. In addition, person A did not eat his meal. If you go to a restaurant and buy a meal, you will eat all of it. This means that person A could have been the one shot. Person A was point-blank range from the handprint left on the wall. Also, the footprints labeled X are facing to the left. When your right hand is against the wall, your foot will be pointed to the left. This makes me believe that footprints X are the killers. One of the last pieces of evidence is footprint Z goes into the kitchen. Only the workers go into the kitchen, so that means that Ernie went into the kitchen.

The evidence does show and support what the witness has reported. First of all, since the killer had his right hand on the wall then his feet would be pointed to the left and footprint X are facing to the left and go in the right direction. Also, person C's silverware are on the left side so that means he is left handed and the shooter is left handed. Person A's chair is point blank range so this is even more evidence.

This evidence leads me to believe that Person C is guilty. We reached this conclusion because person C is left handed due to his silverware being on the left side of his plate. Also, the killer had his right hand on the wall so that means he had to shoot with his left hand. So all to the evidence is pointing toward person C.

Image 5.7 Sample Police Report

As a way to close and reflect on the unit, I like to have my students share their reports orally with the rest of the class and see what kinds of evidence was discovered with each group, what their claims were, and the conclusions they have drawn from the mystery. By listening to one another's report, it generates a great classroom discussion and it allows the students to reflect back on what they did and see ways they could have improved.

This particular report is crucial when they move into writing a written report for the salmon project they participate in throughout the year, described more in chapter 7. The scaffolding that is done helps put the students at ease and they feel more confident writing in the genre of argument.

Cross Content Area Connections

As we have known for many years, and as the Common Core makes clear, learning how to write is more than just the business of the English teacher. So, when we think about writing arguments in other classes, we need to help our students understand what "counts" as evidence in different disciplines (Table 5.5). While this list is by no means complete (as Troy and I are definitely "English nerds"), we hope that it provides a good place to begin conversations with your colleagues about how you might collaborate to teach argument writing across the disciplines. Two books that will offer you more background on these issues are Jetton and Shanahan's *Adolescent Literacy in the Academic Disciplines: General Principles and Practical Strategies* (2012) and Conley et al.'s *Meeting the Challenge of Adolescent Literacy: Research We Have, Research We Need* (2008).

Table 5.5 Cross-Disciplinary Comparison of Different Types of Evidence

Science	Social Studies	Math	Art, Music
• Testable hypothesis • Accurate measurement • Ability to replicate • Drawing appropriate conclusions from data	• Primary and secondary source documents • Background information about the era, people, and place • Using relevant statistics or data	• Explanation of a correct answer or a mathematical concept with appropriate reasoning	• Interpreting colors, shapes, artistic movements, and symbols • Interpreting intonation, tone, balance, blend, and rhythms
• For all: defining key terms and using disciplinary vocabulary effectively			

Where Do They Go Now?

Argument writing is my last big unit I do with my students in the terms of genres. There are two other very useful websites that you will want to consider when helping your students discover topics and think about good mentor texts for argument:

- Room for Debate Blog: www.nytimes.com/roomfordebate
- ProCon.org: www.procon.org

Now that students have had a taste of what it is like to write within all three of the required genres of the CCSS, I want my students to carry forward and use what they have learned. The next two chapters will explore the tools that can help you get your students to become better speakers and listeners (chapter 6) and visual literacy (chapter 7). Finally, students complete a multigenre research project (chapter 8). Because I don't want my students to just simply write in one specific genre and forget about it, I have developed my own version of a multigenre project based on ones created by Tom Romano, Camille Allen, and Melinda Putz, teacher authors I will introduce in the next chapter. Let's continue the journey.

 6 Can You Hear Me Now? (Speaking and Listening)

Like . . . umm . . . yeah! OMG!

Sound familiar? Students are speaking and listening all the time, mostly to each other, but also when we are in front of the class lecturing or giving directions. Or at least we hope they are listening. As it always has been, the challenge that remains for us as teachers is that there may be speaking and listening going on all the time, yet there are a few opportunities for formal speaking and listening within our classrooms. Students listen and speak every day, whether it is in our classroom or in the hallways. After all, isn't it a daily occurrence to see students walking down hallways with headphones or earbuds in their ears listening to music prior to a sporting event or before and after school?

As educators we may not often think about how our students are programmed. In a world with so many distractions, students are learning how to juggle many different tasks at one time. For instance, my principal was telling me a story about his oldest son and how he was sitting on the couch one evening at home; he had the television on, his laptop open to his Facebook page, and was texting on his phone. He was doing all of this while listening to what his father had to say to him. The fascinating aspect about this whole scenario is that he knew who was saying what and how he needed to respond to each individual. In this sense, he was listening to multiple channels of information and processing them all at once.

Or did he?

Although it seems that students are able to hold multiple conversations in their head and across various devices, there is more and more research to prove that our brains are not as effective at multitasking as we might think.

For instance, Annie Murphy Paul reports on the work of a professor at California State University-Dominguez Hills, Larry Rosen, who argues that there are many consequences on our attention and memory when we multitask. For students, in particular, assignments take longer and mental fatigue sets in faster, and they have difficulty processing and storing information (Murphy Paul, 2013). There are numerous other academic studies and anecdotal reports that demonstrate the effect that multitasking has on our overall attention, and most of them indicate that we might be losing our focus, literally and figuratively. Given that we have written an entire book on the positive aspects that technology can play in the language arts classroom and in students' lives, we are not as likely to simply agree that "Google is making us stupid" (Carr, 2008) or that we are teaching "the dumbest generation" (Bauerlein, 2008) as some popular article and book titles would have us believe. But, no doubt, something is happening with the way that our students communicate.

So, as educators and parents, both Troy and I feel that teaching students how to listen and speak are skills that are just as important as any of the other language arts skills discussed in this book. These are both life skills and curricular standards. The state of Michigan, for instance, has had listening and speaking standards embedded in the language arts standards since the mid-1990s. In fact, there was talk at one time of creating a listening and speaking portion of the state's standardized test, the MEAP (it was abandoned because they could not figure out how to effectively distribute audio to every school and also record audio from every student as a speaking sample). Of course, for our purposes in this book, we are paying more attention to the CCSS, which breaks listening and speaking into two main activities:

- Comprehension and collaboration, in which students participate in small group discussions, setting goals, adhering to norms, posing and responding to particular questions.
- Presentation of knowledge and ideas, in which students prepare an organized description with sufficient examples and appropriate speaking behaviors, including multimedia components and visual displays.

We would characterize this as the difference between "speaking and listening to learn" and "speaking and listening to demonstrate learning." In the first—using speaking and listening to learn—we want students to demonstrate their abilities to both participate in and synthesize a conversation. This is a highly important skill not only for class discussions but also if we want them to be actively engaged in literature circles or peer response writing groups. In the second—using speaking and listening to demonstrate learning—we are interested in having students become clear and articulate speakers, ready to respond to the needs of their audience, both by preparing effective presentations as well as listening carefully to their audience for misunderstandings, questions, or the need for elaboration. Often, this kind of careful listening requires both verbal and nonverbal cues, a skill set that our students are still mastering.

We know that speaking and listening are incredibly important. At some level, in some manner, everyone wants to be heard as well as know their voice influences others. For my middle school students, I see that they often enter middle school with a lack of confidence in their own voice. Students light up when they know that they are going to speak to their peers and, more importantly, know that their peers are going to truly listen. By being thoughtful about speaking and listening, and teaching my students everything from classroom norms such as how to speak during a class discussion to more formal situations such as how to address an adult when presenting a problem, we can address issues such as code switching and how to change tone for different audiences and purposes.

In order to meet these types of requirements for listening and speaking, I will describe two types of activities. For comprehension and collaboration, or speaking and listening to learn, I'll explain how I've adapted Harvey Daniels's idea of "literature circles" (2002), using a number of technologies to support students as they interact with one another and the text. For presentation of knowledge and ideas, or speaking and listening to demonstrate learning, I'll talk about the eighth grade exit speech that we use as a form of assessment at the middle school level.

Two final notes before jumping into some speaking and listening strategies. First, Kristen Swanson, a fellow Eye on Education author, has created *Teaching the Common Core Speaking and Listening Standards: Strategies and Digital Tools* (2013), a book worth checking out for its numerous possibilities, which we cannot fully delve into in this chapter. Second, another book that might be of interest as you think about communicating more in our digital world is Sherry Turkle's *Alone Together: Why We Expect More from Technology and Less from Each Other* (2011); also see her TED Talk about the book. Listening and speaking through face-to-face communication must remain a critical part of the human experience, and Turkle points out the ways that technology might inadvertently be playing a negative role in our relationships. For instance, some of my students wanted to deliver their exit speeches, discussed later in the chapter, at home with a flip video camera. They did not want to get up in front of their peers to speak. I wanted to help them feel "uncomfortable" so they learn how to deal with the anxiety of public speaking. While we may not agree with everything in her approach to showing how communication is changing our relationships—because we do find that many technologies can be used with purpose—she certainly raises a key point about how we interact with one another. Let's look at some ways to encourage our students on how speaking and listening can be scaffolded in the language arts classroom.

Digital Literature Circles

SL.7.1—Engage effectively in a range of collaborative discussions (one-on-one, in groups, and teacher-led) with diverse partners on grade 7 topics, texts, and issues, building on others' ideas and expressing their own clearly.

First introduced in the mid-1990s by Harvey Daniels, the idea of literature circles has grown in the past two decades to become a significant teaching practice in language arts classes. Daniels's book, *Literature Circles: Voice and Choice in the Student-Centered Classroom* (2002), is the resource I have leaned on for the past two years. He argues,

> When implemented as they were originally conceived, literature circles have the potential to transform power relationships in the classroom, to make kids both more responsible for and more in control of their own education, to unleash lifelong readers, and to nurture critical, personal stance toward ideas. (2002, p. 31)

Literature circles can be defined as small groups consisting of three to five students who are reading the same book. "So two potent ideas—independent reading and cooperative learning come together in the elegant and exciting classroom activity called literature circles" (Daniels, 2002, p. 12).

Defining a single purpose for literature circles is difficult because there can be multiple purposes, and any teacher could have different reasons for using them in the classroom. In making connections to speaking and listening, one of my objectives is for students to work in a collaborative setting to build speaking skills with their peers, while making personal connections with a text. Second, I want my students to take responsibility for reading on their own and developing effective ways to have discussions with their classmates instead of me, their teacher, doing it for them.

Most importantly, I want to step away from the typical classroom discussion of a book where the teacher has generated questions and he or she asks the class as a whole and the same three or four students answer the questions. I have done this in the past and have seen the error of my ways. I want students to think creatively and think of their own ideas where they maintain conversation frameworks with their peers.

Literature circles are much more than an alternate way for students to read. The table below paraphrases the roles mentioned in Daniels's book, updated with some digital tools that I will discuss in this chapter. There are three to four students per group. Within each group there are six different "jobs" that are shared during the time the students are reading. Students rotate jobs so that they all experience each one. Table 6.1 explains each job that I have adopted for my classrooms. My job descriptions mirror Daniels's in some aspects, but I have adapted them to my own classroom. In addition, I have described the digital tools that accompany each job. Incorporation of the digital tools offers the students a chance to communicate outside of the classroom and work on each of their individual responsibilities. Later in the chapter, I have offered a more detailed description of what my expectations are for each job.

A writing project colleague, Shannon Powell, and her technology director, Amy Meinhardt, shared the idea of digital literature circles with me. I specifically like the idea of students being exposed to multiple texts or novels, because it is difficult to have students read many different books. Furthermore, students have a choice in what they are reading, which helps to turn students, especially the boys in my classroom, on to reading more.

To begin, I start literature circles by spending a class period having a book preview day. I start by laying out the books we will be using for the unit. The books are located at five or six different locations throughout my room and that can depend on how many books you want your students to explore. Students are equipped with a laptop, guidelines for the book preview, a sheet that has QR codes, and a link to a survey created using Cel.ly that they must complete at the end. The QR codes are linked to digital book trailers on the titles I have chosen. The book trailer can help the students make a decision about what book they want to read. They scan the QR code (see Image 6.1) to see a book trailer on the book *Hoot* by Carl

Table 6.1 Roles in Digital Literature Circles

Job Title	Responsibility	Digital Tool
Discussion Manager	The individual who keeps everyone on track and creates the discussion questions for the day. Creates questions for group discussion that comes from his or her own thoughts and feelings. Such a question might be, What was surprising during this section of reading?	Cel.ly: social networking tool for students to collaborate in created cells
Summarizer	Prepares a summary of the section of reading that was assigned. Students should only highlight main ideas by writing perhaps no more than six to eight sentences per paragraph, no longer than a half page. The students create short videos of themselves doing a summary of the given reading assignment.	Flip camera: for recording digital video (alternatively, could use smartphone); posts to YouTube
Vocabulary	Pulls out new vocabulary terms that may be important. Student locates hard to pronounce, puzzling, or unfamiliar words to discuss with group. Student creates online flash cards that everyone else can access.	Quizlet: free tool for creating flashcards
Illustrator	Creates a scene in the book. Draws pictures related to the reading. For instance, the student composes a drawing of the main character.	Toondoo: users can create comics and cartoons Pixton: comic creator with more posable characters
Passage (Picker) Pointer	Finds a meaningful passage from his or her section of the story and read it aloud to the other group members. Student picks out funny, troubling, interesting, or parts that highlight good writing. Student creates a podcast for this job.	Audacity: free audio editor used to edit and record sound Soundcloud: free online audio recorder
Connection Maker	Makes a real world connection to the book, be it to real life, another piece of fiction, or the like.	Wikispaces: free Web-hosting service Student shares various links to Web pages with the group

Image 6.1 QR Code for Book Trailer

1. *Uglies* by Scott Westerfield (2011): A quality girl's read that is science fiction and because there is a series, it tempts and challenges the readers to explore more reading. (8th)

2. *Million-Dollar Throw* by Mike Lupica (2010): Clearly a book about sports and very appealing to boys. (7th)

3. *Hoot* by Carl Hiaasen (2005): Because I want to expose my students to quality writing, this Newberry Honor book does just that and is humorous, which middle school students enjoy. (7th)

4. *The Call of the Wild* by Jack London (1903): Again, I am trying appeal to my boy readers with this choice. In addition, I deem this as a classic read that can grab some of my readers due to the fact we have already read the short story "To Build a Fire" by London. (8th)

5. *Out of the Dust* by Karen Hesse (1997): My 7th graders early on learn about visual literacies and the pictures from the dust bowl, so they have some prior knowledge. This Newberry Award Winning book springboards from our lessons with visual literacies and the book offers a unique perspective from a young girl during this time period. (8th)

6. *The Transall Saga* by Gary Paulsen (1998): The students are exposed to Gary Paulsen's style of writing in elementary school and the 7th graders see him again in a short story in our literature book. Many students are lured to this book because they recognize the author. Students are surprised when the story turns sci-fi! (8th)

Figure 6.1 Books Used with Seventh and Eighth Grade
Literature Circles in 2012–2013

Hiaasen, found on YouTube. Figure 6.1 is a list of a few of the books I used in the 2011–2012 school year with both seventh and eighth grade with a brief explanation next to each of them.

Cel.ly is the social networking tool that is great for organizing, collaborating, and getting students to think critically, especially during digital literature circles. Every student is going to have a different response because each student in the group is going to have a different job. For instance, the Investigator in the group is going to post something completely different from the Discussion Director.

Now, when the students post to Cel.ly, they must put their job title before they respond, and they must write complete sentences without convention or grammar errors. If students do not have a cell phone, they can use the phone of one of their group's members, or they can use our classroom wiki and go to the discussion page. The students are engaged, and it generates not only verbal conversation within the literature circle, but ongoing collaboration extends beyond the classroom when students discuss the book while at home doing their reading assignment.

Within the groups, each student takes a copy of the title in front of them and has about seven minutes to look at the book, watch the book trailer, and complete the survey. The survey asks the following:

- title
- author
- interest level: scale of 1 to 10, 10 being the highest
- one sentence describing what they think the book is about

After their time is up, the students rotate groups and do the same thing with the next book that is in front of them. When students are finished with all six books, I have them rate their choices on a scale so they can potentially read their top choice. I explain to the students they may not get their first choice, but I can guarantee they will get something within their top three. I take their sheets and, after class, start organizing students into literature circle groups. Students are grouped based on interest, and if there are more people interested than the number of books I have, they receive their second choice. From here, I introduce to them the idea of completing their literature circles digitally and their jobs.

Creating a Wikispace Page for Each Digital Literature Circle

A wiki page can be made with all of the groups' books on it in a table, and then each group can fill in their table with links to their jobs. A Wikispace is a collaborative web space where students or teachers and students can hold discussions and collaborate on projects, and use as a platform to post work. It is free for educators to use; you just need an e-mail and a password to create a wiki.

In the past, I have created a classroom wiki as a means to collaborate with my students and conduct engaging discussions. In addition, I have had students create their own pages within a wiki where they could house their writing (see Images 6.2 and 6.3). In essence, they created a portfolio where

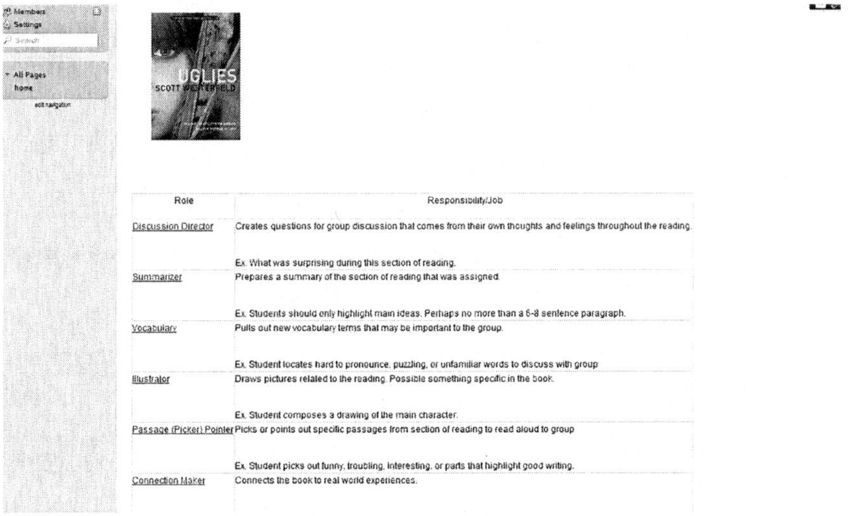

Role	Responsibility/Job
Discussion Director	Creates questions for group discussion that comes from their own thoughts and feelings throughout the reading. Ex. What was surprising during this section of reading.
Summarizer	Prepares a summary of the section of reading that was assigned. Ex. Students should only highlight main ideas. Perhaps no more than a 6-8 sentence paragraph.
Vocabulary	Pulls out new vocabulary terms that may be important to the group. Ex. Student locates hard to pronounce, puzzling, or unfamiliar words to discuss with group
Illustrator	Draws pictures related to the reading. Possible something specific in the book. Ex. Student composes a drawing of the main character.
Passage (Picker) Pointer	Picks or points out specific passages from section of reading to read aloud to group. Ex. Student picks out funny, troubling, interesting, or parts that highlight good writing.
Connection Maker	Connects the book to real world experiences.

Image 6.2 Screenshot from the Digital Literature Circle Page for *Uglies*

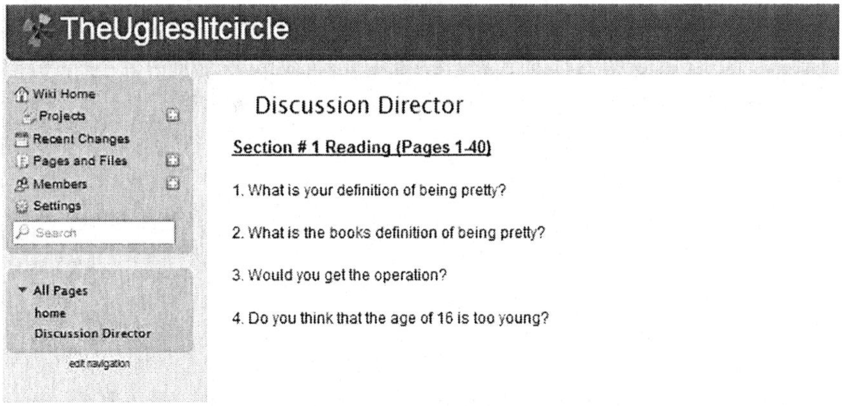

Image 6.3 Screenshot from the Digital Literature Circle Page for *Uglies*

I could visit their work at any time and see how each student was growing as writers over the course of the year. Troy and I have even used a wiki as our resource page for this book (createcomposeconnect.wikispaces.com). I want my students to create a wiki for their literature circles in order to engage in thoughtful conversations while reading the book and demonstrate their understanding and comprehension of the text they have chosen. Furthermore, I can monitor their progress as they are reading. It is a way for me to make sure they are carrying out their job responsibilities.

Defining Roles in the Digital Literature Circle Group

Below, I describe the roles introduced in Table 6.1 in more detail.

Discussion Manager

This student creates questions for the assigned reading. As Daniels explains in his book, the student should develop questions from their "own thoughts, feelings, and concerns"(Daniels, 2002). Personally I feel this individual is the leader of group for the given section of reading. He or she keeps everyone on task and helps to move the conversation along if it stalls out. I ask the Discussion Managers to post questions on the wiki prior to class and ask them to send it to their group members via Cel.ly.

The requirement for the Discussion Managers is to post the questions on their cell in Cel.ly prior to the next day's discussion. This is done every other day. Students need time to be able to discuss what they are reading. I encourage students to post questions and comments from Cel.ly to the wiki page if they feel it is beneficial to the group. This gives the students time to think about the questions and enhance the group's discussion on the following day. The discussion manager posts the questions to the wiki the day of the discussion. This is the beginning to meeting standard SL.7.1 where students are having collaborative discussions with a text.

Summarizer

The title speaks for itself. The Summarizer completes a half-page summary and posts it to the wiki. Also, the students complete a recording of themselves giving the summary. The student can read from the one they wrote or simply paraphrase it. The Summarizers posts their recording to the wiki for participating group members to watch and refer back to when it comes time to prepare for potential assessments, such as tickets-out-the-door, quizzes, or tests. By students creating a video recording, they are practicing comprehension and collaboration, which was mentioned at the beginning of the chapter, by participating in a group discussion with their peers.

Vocabulary Improvement

This job requires the student in charge to find words that are new, confusing, or do not make sense. I require the student in charge to find at least six words in each section of reading. Then, the student reports back to the group each discussion day with the words. They use Quizlet, mentioned in chapter 2, as an online vocabulary tool; it is free and easy to sign up to and use. It is also available as an app for iOS and Android. Quizlet has some amazing features where the students can not only create flash cards, but they can also save them on the Web site and come back to them at a later time to pick up where they left off. It also has an audio feature where students can have the words read to them out loud in case they are having difficulty with pronunciation. Furthermore, students can use the "speller" option on the site. For example, an elementary teacher may want to use the site for spelling and spelling practice. When the student finishes the flash cards he or she will then share with the other group members for discussion and study purposes.

Personally I like how the site has some game options for learning the words. With middle school students, especially my boys who like to play games, this allows me to tell them they can play the games that correspond with terms given; that way, they don't even know they are studying. Besides middle or elementary school, I can see real potential for ACT and SAT prep with this particular tool.

Passage (Picker) Pointer

Students give their explanation about a particular part in the book. Students turn this into a podcast. There are free audio recording apps and software you can use. I personally like Audacity. It is free and easy to use. It can be uploaded to where you want it placed. For example, my students upload their recording to the Wikispace. Vocaroo is another free online tool that allows you to record and save your recordings. Students can also keep their video or audio recording in their digital portfolio on Google Drive. There are other apps available on smartphones that can create recordings, too.

Illustrator

In Daniels's book, the Illustrator is instructed to draw a picture related to the reading. With digital literature circles, the students use Toondoo (toondoo. com) to create a scene from the book to bring to the discussion. There are unlimited drawing sites available. Toondoo is a free digital tool where students can create cartoons or comic strips. The students particularly like the creativity involved in using this resource. The Web site only requires an e-mail address, user name, and password. Pixton (pixton.com) is another comic strip tool available. Pixton has age restrictions on it and could cause potential issues for certain students. For instance, students will not be able to save a comic they create because they don't meet the age requirement. It may result in another parent permission slip being sent home if your students don't meet the age requirement. With Toondoo, the students make a four-pane comic strip and share their creation with their group. The other students respond and make comments about the illustration and the scene. I implement this job in my classroom because I think there is value in visual literacy (chapter 7).

Connection Maker

This person tries to make a real world connection between the book to something of outside it, maybe to real life, another piece of fiction, or something else. Students create hot links (to the author's site, more info on topics in the book, books like it, etc.) that relates to the book. My hope is that the students can make multiple connections with the book they are reading. By making these deeper connections, students accomplish a deeper comprehension of their reading. Also, it stimulates conversation that goes beyond the text. Students are not just answering questions but also thinking critically about where the author got his or her ideas, the messages the author was trying to convey to the reader, and whether or not the book could be adapted into a movie.

Image 6.4 shows a Connection Maker's wiki page for *The Uglies* where she made a link to the author's blog and, in addition, a link to find out more information about the author. Furthermore, the Connection Maker included a few of the book's themes and embedded a trailer from YouTube for a movie adaptation. She also included a visual of another book that is related to the book her group is reading. Students already have a basic knowledge of how to create links and embed video into their pages because of the walk-through I do with them at the start of the unit.

Image 6.4 Screenshot of the Connection Maker's page on the Wikispace

Final Thoughts on Digital Literature Circles

This is just the basic structure of what digital lit circles look like. There are a plethora of possibilities for each of these tasks, and every week a new program or app comes out that might enhance and make literature circles better. The implementation of this strategy can be varied from teacher to teacher. I like the idea of the students discussing books through tools like Cel.ly or the discussion board on Schoology. Students who are less likely to speak up in a small group discussion or whole class discussion are given an opportunity to give responses and are more likely to say something or speak up about the book being discussed. In my short experience with using online collaborative sites, there is more student participation because students feel more comfortable sharing their ideas because they don't actually have to talk.

However, I don't think using collaborative spaces should completely replace having face-to-face conversations. Though reluctant students are more likely to respond in Web-based spaces, students also need to experience face-to-face conversations and collaboration where there may be the potential for uncomfortable silence and confrontation. Face-to-face conversations teach students to actively engage with one another and can have the lasting effect of building trust among peers when it comes to expressing thoughts verbally instead of hiding behind written words on a collaborative online space. In a world with so many distractions, I make it a norm for my students to have nothing in their hands when others are speaking. In addition, I want them to face whoever is speaking during a class discussion. This takes practice, patience, and multiple reminders from me to teach proper listening skills to students. If students are sitting with their back to the person who is speaking and doodling in their notebooks, they aren't listening or comprehending what their classmate is saying. As mentioned at the beginning of the chapter, when dealing with comprehension and collaboration, I want my students to actively participate in discussions. This means they are going to have to ask questions and respond to not only me but also their classmates.

Exit Speeches

At the end of their eighth grade year, my students prepare for the "big one," the one that would still make some adults nervous: the exit speech! (See Table 6.2.)

Every year as my eighth graders get their own version of senior fever, I introduce them to one of their final assignments before they enter high school: the exit speech. The exit speech essentially is a reflection of the whole middle school experience. As you have been reading throughout this book, I believe it is important for students to reflect on the assignments they complete. The exit speech not only gives the students a chance to reflect back on their whole year, but it can provide next year's eighth graders with some sound advice for surviving another year with the middle school teachers and potentially drive them to reflect back on what they need to change from seventh grade to help them be more successful as they inch closer to high school.

Table 6.2 MAPS for Exit Speeches

Mode	Formal speech
Media	Prepared notes, presentation, podcast
Audience(s)	Classmates, teachers, principal
Purpose(s)	Students prepare an organized description using sufficient examples and appropriate speaking behaviors, including multimedia components and visual displays. Reflective component about the skills that students have learned. Using a "hook" to capture the audiences attention.
Situation	The presentation much be two to three minutes and include visuals. Listeners must create three questions for the speaker.

SL.7.1—Engage effectively in a range of collaborative discussions (one-on-one, in groups, and teacher-led) with diverse partners on grade 7 topics, texts, and issues, building on others' ideas and expressing their own clearly.

In addition to providing an opportunity for reflection, this assignment also gives students another chance to complete a presentation (their speech) of knowledge and ideas in which they prepare an organized and descriptive form of speaking with sufficient examples and appropriate speaking behaviors, including multimedia components and visual displays. As mentioned earlier in the chapter, this is one of the primary activities in the CCSS for speaking and listening.

I want my students to move beyond PowerPoint presentations; it is not that I don't like PowerPoint presentations, but there are a lot of presentation tools that can be more appealing. By the time my students get to me, they have been using PowerPoint for some time, and they have seen many PowerPoint presentations by their peers. I encourage my students to use tools such as Animoto, Glogster, Prezi, or even Google Presentation (Google Presentation emulates a traditional PowerPoint, but I feel the students can include more creative elements). In addition, Haiku Deck is a free iPad application that can be used to enhance presentations. I want to challenge my students and have them deliver presentations that are appealing and catch their audiences' attention. Visuals can be very effective tools and can thus enhance my students' speeches.

To help students better understand the importance of visuals with speaking, I do video journals with them using TED Talks and Ignite Talk Videos. Many of the speakers in the videos use visuals to help highlight their key points and to keep their audience interested. This gives me the opportunity to talk to the students about the importance of visuals because they

- help the speaker stay on task with main points;
- highlight and accentuate the speaker's key points;
- draw in and keep the audience's attention; and
- appeal to visual learners.

For example, in Image 6.5 a student name Lauren created a Prezi. Her visual is not only appealing, but she also uses the idea of the tree and its

Image 6.5 The introduction slide to Lauren's Prezi

branches to help her remember the main points of her speech. The Prezi allowed her to move from point to point as she worked her way through the speech. Furthermore, as she was reflecting back on her speech she wanted the visual to emulate how her class is continuing to grow like a tree with new branches of experience every year. As an audience member, I was not only drawn in but also intrigued by how she placed her key points at the end of each branch. Lauren did a phenomenal job using a visual with her speech. Image 6.6 shows a closer look at Lauren's Prezi and the specific branches.

Also, to help better explain visuals to my students, I even discuss my own experiences of delivering professional development. I tell my students that if I didn't have student examples to share with participants, they would not be able to see how a particular unit, lesson, or activity works in the classroom. In chapter 7, more detail is given on how students watch TED Talks and Ignite videos while critically thinking about how presenters use different visuals to enhance their presentations.

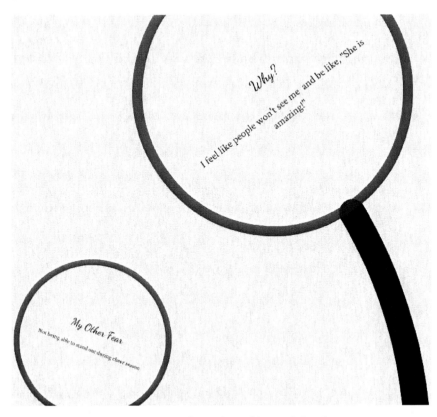

Image 6.6 A closer view of Lauren's Prezi

SL.8.4—Present claims and findings, emphasizing salient points in a focused, coherent manner with relevant evidence, sound, valid reasoning, and well-chosen details; use appropriate eye contact, adequate volume, and clear pronunciation.

As my students are thinking about visuals, I show my eighth graders a very cheesy, out-of-date VHS video about giving effective classroom speeches. After this year, I am going to have to find something else for them to watch because the tape quality has become so poor. Still, I show them the video because I want my students to understand how much delivering a formal speech has changed over the years. What do I mean by this? Think with me for a moment back to high school or middle school. How did your teacher want you to stand in front of the class? Arms down, eyes on your audience, and no movement! Am I right? The video asks the same of students, and I quickly point out that speeches just aren't given in that manner any more. Honestly, have you ever seen a teacher standing behind the podium for an entire lecture? Effective teachers move around while talking to their students; they interact with the audience.

The grainy video proves to be effective; it discusses bringing in props, and although that does happen on occasion, most people stick with visual presentations that can be viewed on a screen. After watching a video that shows my students more of what *not* to do, I have them do a quick write-up in Google Docs. I ask them to jot down why they fear public speaking and what strengths they feel they have when it comes to public speaking.

As you can imagine, I get a wide range of answers. In Table 6.3 I have displayed how the students reflected on their own strengths and weaknesses as speakers. In my opinion, their answers accurately reflect middle school students and their mindset.

I assure the students that this mentality is very normal, even for adults. We discuss some strategies for preparing and delivering their speeches, such as following:

- Practice with a friend while timing the speech using a cell phone or stop watch.
- Video record the speech to watch body language and eye contact.
- Practice in front of mirror.
- Digitally voice record the speech in a quiet room using a cell phone and play back the recording to see what needs to be fixed.

Table 6.3 Student Fears and Strengths Related to Public Speaking

Student Fears Related to Public Speaking	Student Strengths Related to Public Speaking
• Classmates won't be interested • Mispronouncing a word • Inability to answer questions that are asked • Stuttering • Forgetting material • Talking too fast • Being judged by peers	• Ability to communicate • Beautiful smile • Interaction with the audience • Knowledge of the audience • Ability to be humorous • Student feels more comfortable because of their experience playing organized sports in front of an audience

Next, I present rubric guidelines. The whole process takes about two weeks to complete. Initially I have the students write an outline based on the guidelines (see Figure 6.2) so I can see what they are thinking. I do like to go over the outline with the student prior to the student completing a full written speech. This requires me to set aside some conferencing time with each student. I give each student two to three minutes to discuss his or her concerns with the speech, and I look specifically at the academic skills they have listed. Students do the academic skills section poorly because they do not provide enough specific detail about what they have learned. For example, most students simply say, "I learned a lot in math class," instead of saying, "I learned how to plot points on a graph correctly." Most students want to discuss a tool or a process instead of a skill. When talking to the students about this, I ask them to think about the skills they could potentially possess for a job or use in more challenging classes when they are in high school. I want them to think in terms of having a job interview and an employer asking them what skills they have that would make the company or person want to hire them. This hits home with the students, and by the time they give their speeches, they tend to do well with this section.

The part students struggle with the most is how to end their speech. They are so nervous they want to just walk off and get back to their seat, or they want to say, "That's it!" while putting their head down and exiting the front of the room. I give my students two bits of advice for ending their speeches.

- Ask if there are any questions, and say thank you.
- End the speech with some words of wisdom.

These two simple suggestions prove to be effective, and the students do feel more confident at the end of their speech.

From here, the students script their speeches. I require this because I want my students to have a solid idea of what they are going to say and not just to jot down a few ideas on notecards. Also, as mentioned earlier, the students have to be detailed, and this gives rise to better content when the students deliver their speech. Students are not required to use the script when they are giving their speech, but I still give them a grade based on content, grammar skills, and so on. I have never had a student walk up to the front of the classroom with a full script nor have I had a student who memorized his or her speech; the latter could be a choice given to students.

Even though the students are not allowed to use their full script, they are allowed to use note cards when they are giving their speeches. Approximately

Exit Speech—Eighth Grade

Purpose: to share experiences from middle school, give advice to future eighth graders, and to share concerns about high school.

Curriculum Connections:

S.L.8.6: Adapt speech to a variety of contexts and tasks, demonstrating command of formal English when indicated or appropriate.

S.L.8.5: Integrate multimedia and visual displays into presentations to clarify information, strengthen claims and evidence, and add interest.

- **I can** integrate an appropriate media component or visual display to improve my presentation. (Such as a short video, Prezi, or Glog). The visual should aid in helping you remember the content of your speech and to help keep your audience's attention.
- **I can** identify various reasons for speaking. Know the difference between formal and non-formal speaking.
- **I can** determine speaking tasks that will require a formal structure.
- **I can** compose a formal speech that demonstrates a command of grade 8 Language standards. This would be your exit speech!

Length: 4–5 minutes (You are allowed to be under by 20 seconds. I do allow you to speak longer, up to one full minute longer). Time yourself when you practice and make the appropriate adjustments.

What the Speech Should Include:

1. Opening statement—discuss your overall middle school experience.
2. Memorable moments—talk about 2–3 of your most memorable moments from middle school. For example, a time you got in trouble, or a touchdown you scored in a football game. Include at least one positive and one negative experience.
3. What important academic skills have you learned that has better prepared you for high school? Discuss at least 2–3 academic skills that your teachers have taught you. Be specific, How are going to use the skill in the future?
4. Talk with your classmates about the concerns you have entering high school? Are you afraid of the rigor? Do you worry about certain teachers or classes?
5. What advice and/or strategies can you give next year's 8th graders to help them be successful? For instance, use their planner, study more, read more, etc.?
6. Closing remarks—restate your opening statement.
7. Speech should include a visual whether it is a Google Presentation, Animoto video, Glog, or Prezi that highlights key discussion points in your speech and keeps your audience intrigued.

* This is a formal speech. I do expect you to dress up.

Boys—dress pants and a collared shirt.

Girls—dress pants, school appropriate dress, etc.

Figure 6.2 Instructions for Exit Speech Assignment

two-thirds of the students use notecards for the speech. I do not require it, but it is an option for them. With them practicing for two whole days, my hope is that they won't need them, but I understand if they want them. I often refer to the notecards as the students' "security blanket." It makes them feel better that they have them, but the notecards aren't really necessary. I warn the students not to use them as a crutch and to remember that the notecards are not their audience, as some students like to bury their faces in the cards when in front of the class. I try to get my students to understand that when they create their notecards, they should write out more of an outline rather than trying to cram in the whole speech, which happens on occasion. I tell them they should just put the key points on the cards as reminders of what to say; otherwise, their noses *are* buried in the notecards during the entire speech. Many teachers may argue that notecards are not needed because of the visual presentations that accompany the students. The use of notecards can be left up to the teacher.

Practice Makes Us Better, Not Perfect

After the students write out their speech, I set aside two whole days for them to practice. During these two days, I equip my students with stopwatches, flip cams, and their laptops. I also allow students to use their own handheld device, such as a cell phone, if they have one available. Students pair up with a partner and find a designated spot to so they can record one another. Once the students have recorded each other, I have them watch their speeches and reflect on what they see. Below is a set of questions I have them consider.

1. Did you maintain eye contact with the person recording?
2. Did you meet the required time limit? Did you exceed it?
3. How many times did you say "umm," "like," or other fillers?
4. Were you loud enough in the video to emulate how you will actually deliver your speech?
5. What can you do to make your speech better?
6. How could you have improved on your visual? Was it appealing, and did it help get your main ideas across?

The six questions are enough to help the student improve without making them feel overwhelmed. By giving the students two class periods, each one can practice twice and gain more confidence in his or her speaking skills.

Upon completing the second day of practice, I encourage students to practice again at home on their own. Additionally, I sign students up for their speeches. I ask for volunteers first, and then I just draw names out of a hat.

Special Delivery

Because I teach in a smaller school district and I have smaller class sizes, I can get away with using two whole class periods when students deliver their actual speech. I require the students to dress up. The boys in my class typically have a fit about this, but I still ask them to wear a nice pair of pants and a collared shirt. I require the girls in my class to look formal, too. I do not allow my students to wear jeans or flip-flops during their speeches. I do take into consideration students who may not have certain items because of their financial situation. I usually grade them accordingly.

On the day the students deliver their speeches, I sit at an empty student desk as if I were one of their peers. I time them with a stopwatch; there are also free online timers you can use. Every 30 seconds I hold up a notecard with the time on it so the speaker can see how much time he or she has remaining to meet the 4 to 5 minute requirement. Again, I find this is helpful to the students because it teaches them how to be detailed yet concise enough to get their points across to their intended audience without them rambling on while they are speaking. They speak about their main points without being too wordy and wasting the time they have to deliver their speech.

Also, as the students are delivering the speech I fill out a rubric (see the resource page on our wiki: createcomposeconnect.wikispaces.com). It is broken down into four categories, and I am able to quickly give feedback on how each student has done, and they get a quick turnaround on seeing their grade. Each day of the speeches, generally 8 to 10 students deliver speeches. I suggest not going any higher than 10 to prevent restlessness among audience members. Talking to your students about being good audience members is helpful, too. Students can be good audience members by

- remembering they will be in front of the classroom, too;
- making eye contact with the speaker;
- positioning their body so they are facing the speaker; and
- engaging with the speaker by asking questions.

The students are genuinely well-behaved and respectful of those who appear more nervous getting up in front of others.

Upon completion of the speeches, I take the ones I have recorded on video and as podcasts and post them so that next year's eighth graders and I can access them when it comes time to do the same assignment. You can find the student samples on our resource site under chapter 6. I have my students listen to the speeches at the beginning of the year to help them get a sense of what they will need to do to be successful in their last year of middle school. It means more for them to hear it from their peers rather than their teacher. If I am measuring growth in my students when it comes to speaking and listening, the exit speech meets the standard discussed at the beginning of the chapter.

- Presentation of knowledge and ideas, in which students prepare an organized description with sufficient examples and appropriate speaking behaviors, including multimedia components and visual displays.

Overall, I feel I am not only meeting curricular needs, but I am also meeting the needs of my students.

What's Next?

While literature circles and exit speeches are specific opportunities for students to practice listening and speaking, there are many other lessons that can foster effective communication skills for my students to show their understanding of how to use formal English. It is also important to remember the informal opportunities. It is easy to assume students know how to handle themselves when talking to a person of authority such as a principal, when it fact, it may be quite unnerving for them. In addition, students need to have the opportunity to learn how to respond to their peers when in class and small group discussions. These skills are not going to be mastered overnight; they are skills that take time to develop much like the skills related to visual literacy, our topic in the next chapter.

Seeing Isn't Always Believing (Visual Literacy)

When being reminded about what it means to be literate in this day and age, visual media certainly comes to mind and plays an important role in literacy. Let's face it, our students are just as likely to record something and post it to YouTube as they are to write a lengthy blog post. Helping them understand when, why, and how to create and share video in critical, creative ways is nearly as important as teaching them how to write an essay.

From grade school to grad school, students are studying a number of visual elements: illustrations in children's books and charts and graphs in non-fiction texts, as well as the intricacies of blending fonts, colors, photographs, and other elements on Web pages, on posters, and in videos. On one level, this is about art and appreciation: What visual elements do we find compelling and beautiful? And, on another level, this is about critical media literacy: What do we need to know about the ways visuals are composed to be a critical consumer? Ours is a visual culture, and teaching students about visual literacy has become a key component of what it means to teach English language arts.

For instance, in the language of the 12 main NCTE/IRA standards, we see phrases such as "print and non-print texts," "textual features," "visual language," and "media techniques" (1996). Woven throughout the many documents about twenty-first century literacies and technologies, we see other indirect references to the impact of visual literacy, too, such as the following phrases from the ISTE NETS for students: "employing a variety of digital environments and media," "process data and report results," and "exhibit leadership for digital citizenship" (2007). Knowing how, when, and why to make the choice between using a picture found online or creating a new one is but one example of the numerous decisions that our digital learners make when it comes to visual literacy. Also, the way that students take and post photos, choose avatars, and remix existing copyrighted material all comes into play, too.

In other words, visual literacy isn't just a fun add-on for students after our "regular" language arts work is done. Rather, understanding and employing visuals is a critical component of what we teach our students. When considering still images, educators such as Burmark (2002), Kajder (2006), Moline (2011), and Ray (2010) give us a variety of entry points into studying visual literacy, both in conjunction with written text as well as a focus of study on its own. Also, a number of graphic designers and business professionals have been advocating for individuals to take more and more responsibility for designing our own documents, slideshows, Web sites, and other digital media because the tools to create these items are easily available and are user friendly. Simple mantras such as Robin Williams's "CRAP" principle make it easy for nondesigners to remember ideas such as contrast, repetition, alignment, and proximity (2008). Other principles, such as Garr Reynolds's "signal vs. noise ratio," the "picture superiority effect," and "empty space" also guide design choices for presentations and other forms of visual media (2008, 2010).

RIT.7.7—Compare and contrast a text to an audio, video, or multimedia version of the text, analyzing each medium's portrayal of the subject (e.g., how the delivery of a speech affects the impact of the words).

While it is outside the scope of this particular chapter to go into too much more detail about video creations such as television, movies, and advertising, I do feel there are some important considerations to take into account. For instance, media scholar Renee Hobbs discusses a variety of ways that visual media affects us, both as consumers and producers. She encourages us to ask five "critical questions" when examining any form of media, and they are particularly applicable in our age of Photoshop and Instagram:

1. Who is the author and what is the purpose?
2. What creative techniques are used to attract and hold attention?
3. How might different people understand the message?
4. What lifestyles, values, and points of view are represented?
5. What is omitted? (Hobbs, 2011, p. 57)

So, as I welcome you into the ways that my students and I explore visual literacy, I will share how my students respond to existing visual content that they can find online, how they remix visual content into new projects, and how they create their own, original content using infographics. As we begin, here is just a brief list of the many types of visuals my students experience over the course of a year, both as consumers and as creators:

- photographs
- slideshows
- Web sites
- charts and graphs

Again, with each of these types of visuals it is not enough to just point my students in the direction of an interesting Web site and tell them to "make a visual." Just as I demonstrate and mentor them throughout the writing process with narrative, informational, and argument genres, I guide them through the process of analyzing existing visuals, as well as creating their own.

Screencasting and Capturing

Before I go into certain tools or lessons where I feel students gain more knowledge and appreciation for visual literacies, I want to discuss the idea of screencasting. The idea of using screencasting and capturing in my classroom goes beyond a blended learning environment where traditional teaching and technology are combined and put into place. I am attracted to the idea of screencasting not only for the visual learners within my classroom, but for the students who are absent that may miss a lesson or the times I am absent and it is more difficult for a substitute teacher to teach a lesson. I am sure there are teachers who share the same anxieties that I do when it comes to being away from the classroom for professional development, sickness, or other personal reasons. As great as our substitute teachers are, nothing keeps our students more focused than seeing their teacher in front of the classroom. Students get used to the idea of us being the leader and guiding them in the right direction. If we can simply screencast a lesson to be played in our absence, we can help our students not lose a beat.

Techsmith offers a number of great tools for screencasting. Their flagship product is Camtasia (www.techsmith.com/camtasia.html). It's pricy but has many features. I prefer to use Snagit, another tool by Techsmith (www.tech-smith.com/snagit.html). Snagit can be purchased for as little as $30.00 if you download it from the Web site. Videos can be saved to YouTube or to screen-cast.com. There is limited space when uploading to screencast. If funding is an issue, Techsmith has another screencast option called Jing (www.techsmith. com/jing.html). Jing can be used for quick mini-lessons. I don't recommend using it for a full-blown lesson unless you want to string together a bunch of videos. Though Jing is free, it only allows you to record five-minute videos. Jing can be a useful tool for reviewing a lesson from the day before or perhaps showing model texts.

Using a tool such as Jing, Snagit, or Camtasia is not only great for when you are absent, but it is also beneficial for students who are absent. I am not suggesting that you record yourself every time you present a new lesson. How-ever, big-unit projects, such as the book review mentioned in chapter 4, can be hard for students to understand. "Mr. Hyler, what did I miss?" used to be a question I dreaded, especially the day after unit projects were presented to the class.

With the above-mentioned tools, I can create a video for students to watch that displays all of the visual prompts I used when I was presenting the day before. Now when a student asks me what he or she missed, I respond by telling him or her to watch the video I posted; teachers can post to places such as Schoology or Wikispaces. If students can't gain access to the video because they don't have Internet access, I can download it onto a flash drive or a write-able disc for them to take home.

Teachers can also capture screenshots for students to view and use to prompt more elaborate discussions. I know at times I myself feel bored if there are no visuals presented to me. There are several different ways a teacher can use images that are screen captured on from the Internet. Creating a screen capture can be as simple as using the snipping tool on a computer or simply pressing the "print screen" button. I personally like using the digital tool Skitch for screen captures (https://evernote.com/skitch).

Skitch was created by the makers of Evernote (chapter 5); it allows you to make marks or drawings on your screen capture with shapes, writing, or stamps. This way you can draw attention to what you want your students to pay attention to. Skitch can be used on multiple devices including iPhones, iPads, laptops, desktops, and Androids. It does require a user name and password, but it is free. If you are already using Evernote, it is easy to access, and your screen captures are shared to your Evernote account. Image 7.1 is a screen capture using Skitch.

How to Complete Mr. Hyler's Article of the Week

I. READ THE ARTICLE (5 points)

Read and have a conversation with the text (annotate). Ask it questions, make comments, point out words or passages you may not know.

    A. Feel free to use symbols. For instance:

        - question marks (?) for questions you have about the reading.
        - exclamation points (!) for something you learned from the text.
        - addition signs (+) for parts of the reading you agree with.
        - subtraction signs (-) for parts of the reading you don't agree with.

    B. Demonstrate evidence of close reading. Mark any other reactions you have as you read. In addition to using symbols, you MUST include writing in the margin. This will help guide your thinking when you are completing the written response at the end.

        - 7th graders - use at least 3 symbols and 3 written reactions on each page.

        - 8th graders - use at least 5 symbols and 5 written reactions on each page.

II. WRITTEN RESPONSE (10 points)

The written response should include the following:

    A. Begin by writing a 4-5 sentence summary about the article (***paragraph #1***). Below is an example of a summary written about a short story that was read. (3 points)

        - In the short story "The Secret Life of Walter Mitty," author James Thurber humorously presents a character who fantasizes about himself as a hero enduring incredibly challenging circumstances. In his real life, Walter Mitty lives an ordinary, plain life; he is a husband under the control of an overbearing, critical wife. Thurber uses lively dialogue to give readers an understanding of Mitty's character. The story takes place over a period of about twenty minutes; during this brief time, Mitty drives his wife to the hairdresser and runs errands that his wife has given him while he waits for her.

Image 7.1 Sample of a Screen Capture Annotated with Skitch

Image 7.1, from the article of the week project I discussed in chapter 4, displays the different features Skitch allows me to use. I can highlight important parts or simply underline them or add arrows pointing to them. In this example, I wanted to point out the importance of annotating the articles. So, I am not only visually showing them what is important, but I have a model for how to properly annotate as well.

The next section in this chapter will elaborate on specific ways visual literacies can be used in the classroom, whether you are using screen capturing tools or simply pulling up an image for students to look at for a journal prompt. Both Troy and I feel we can break down the use of visual literacies into two broad categories: responding to and remixing existing visual content, and creating and sharing new visual content.

Responding to and Remixing Existing Visual Content

There are overwhelming amounts of existing visuals and text that we can utilize as teachers to help our students better understand the lessons and the units we are trying to teach to them. I am confident teachers have used at one time or another a picture or a video when having their students write in their journals. Though I am not going to elaborate on that specific process, I am going discuss some activities for which enhancing visuals already exist.

In terms of visual literacies, oftentimes my students are reading a novel or a short story that offers a rich description of the setting or the events. This opens the door for students to imagine a visual of what's being described. However, for our visual learners, seeing pictures and images of characters, settings, or events can help them comprehend more of their reading. Also, when reading nonfiction, teenagers aren't necessarily going to be wowed by just the words on the page.

Introducing a New Unit or Idea

A simple visual literacy lesson (Table 7.1) I do with my students originated from a seventh grade short story called "The Osage Orange Tree" by William Stafford (2014). The story is set during the time of the Dust Bowl. Because it is hard for my students to visualize what the land was like during this time, I bring in visuals for the students to respond to and think about. A great site with an abundance of pictures from historical events is History Pin (www.historypin.com). Also, you might find some great images in Flickr's The Commons (https://secure.flickr.com/commons).

Table 7.1 MAPS for Visual Response Journal

Mode	Journal entry, written response
Media	Written journal
Audience	Peers and teacher
Purpose	Learning about what pictures can tell us about our past; gaining knowledge about seeing things from someone else's perspective
Situation	The presentation should last two to three minutes and include visuals. Students write a story about what is happening in the picture or tell a story from the perspective of one of the people in the picture.

Image 7.2 Man and Boy Pictured During the Dust Bowl from Library of Congress

From either of these, I can grab pictures such as Image 7.2 by Arthur Rothstein, which is available from the Library of Congress (Rothstein, 1936). Photographs tell stories about our past, and this is exactly what I want my students to try and figure out. For instance, what story can be told about the Dust Bowl here? In addition, I can put a twist on a simple writing response, whether it is in their physical journal or their online journal they have created through Google Docs, by having the students tell a story from the little boy's perspective. This helps the students see events and ideas through the eyes of others.

Though the lesson is very simple, students get a better idea of what the conditions were like during this time, and it helps them understand that the people who lived during this time had plenty of stories to tell.

Developing Deeper Connections to a Text

A more complex example (Table 7.2) comes from my eighth graders, who read for the first time this year *Anne Frank: The Diary of a Young Girl* (1952). *Challenging* and *controversial* are only two of many adjectives that describe this text. The eighth graders come into this reading with solid background knowledge of the Holocaust, the Jewish religion, and World War II from their reading in sixth grade of *Number the Stars* by Lois Lowry (1989). I have to spend less

Table 7.2 MAPS for Developing Deeper Text Connections

Mode	Journal entry
Media	Book covers, curated collections of pictures, virtual tours
Audience	Peers, teachers
Purpose	To help students understand the lessons we can learn through history and for them to understand that Anne Frank had the same teenage tendencies that they do today.
Situation	Students study pictures and images at the beginning of the unit and think about how the pictures and images portray life and what the pictures tell us.

Image 7.3 Anne Frank Image from Wikipedia

than half a class period discussing one of the first activities I do with my students, which is for them to study and analyze the picture of Anne Frank on the front of the book (Image 7.3). I have the students write down their observations in their journals. I give them five minutes to do this. A few student responses can be found below.

- Her clothes are old/out of style.
- She isn't attractive.
- She has a big smile.
- Her hair seems uncombed.
- She seems happy.

After the students share their observations, I put up a random picture of a cover of any popular magazine that has a model on it (an appropriate picture, obviously). I find this image by using Google Images. It's interesting to find pictures with Google Images or the like, but sometimes it is nice to see something that has been curated, too. One resource that has been brilliantly put together is called the Nat Geo Tumblr (http://natgeofound.tumblr.com). The site features a new picture every day that has been taken by a National Geographic photographer. More specifically, for the Anne Frank unit, I like annefrank.org because students can see plenty of pictures of Anne and her family and the Secret Annex where they were hiding, as well as other World War II photos. I specifically like the virtual walk students can take through the Secret Annex.

The idea behind the activity with the photos is to discuss the different perceptions students have based on their initial viewing of a photo or picture. I want my students to think about how easy it is to judge people before they truly get to know them. My hope is that they take our discussion and apply it to their own lives.

As we wrap up our reading and assessment of her diary, we revisit the front cover of our book and the picture of Anne Frank. The students reflect back on the reading and what they have learned about Anne Frank and what she did during her time in hiding. Again, I give them five minutes to write. The responses show an immense amount of change.

- She goes to school and likes math.
- She fights with her mom, like I do.
- She likes to hang out with her friends.
- She thinks about sex.
- She likes food.

What I hope my students understand is that this girl they spend so much time reading about was going through the same things that they are. By having the students go back and write about the picture again, I hope they are able to make some connections between themselves and Anne Frank, despite the fact that the story is over 70 years old and took place in one of the worst circumstances in history.

Analyzing Video Texts

In addition to existing picture content that one can access on the Internet, I enjoy sharing with my students the many TED (Technology, Entertainment,

Table 7.3 MAPS for Analyzing Videos

Mode	Journal writing, class discussion, sharing with a partner
Media	TED Talks, online videos, YouTube videos
Audience	Peers, teachers
Purpose	Students gain an understanding of the importance of using visuals in speeches and presentations.
Situation	Students watch a short TED Talk video or other video that may be found online and think critically about how and why visuals are important in presentations. Students record their thinking in their journal.

and Design) Talks that are available (Table 7.3). Started in 1984, TED is a non-profit organization that aims to spread ideas worth hearing around the world. The Web site is free, and you can register to bookmark all of the videos you want to keep for later use. Prior to my eighth graders doing their exit speeches (chapter 6), I show them a TED Talk by a 12-year-old girl named Adora Svitak (www.ted.com/talks/adora_svitak.html), who speaks about creativity and the importance of letting children be childish when it comes to being creative. When I show my students TED Talks, I want them to make connections with the way the speakers use visuals and what impacts those visuals have on the audience. So, as students are watching the short presentation by Svitak, I want them to think about how she represents her ideas visually through her use of Prezi and write down their findings in their journal.

Throughout the year and not just prior to their speeches, I want my students to think critically about why they may choose certain pictures or images for any of their projects. I don't want them choosing something visual just for the sake of it being cool. They should be thinking about how it relates to their speech or project. In addition, they should consider how the visuals relate to a topic they may be discussing. Furthermore, students should be thinking about who their audience members are and how they can capture their audience's attention with the visuals they choose. As their teacher, I feel this is one area where the students can express their creativity, especially after watching a short TED Talk on creativity.

Mapping Mythical Worlds

To make content and curriculum richer, I am constantly trying to find ways to have my students make connections to other content areas they are studying.

Table 7.4 MAPS for Myth Map Making

Mode	Travelogue
Media	Google Maps, MapQuest
Audience	Peers, teachers, parents passing in the hall (where maps can be displayed)
Purpose	For students to gain a greater understanding of the culture surrounding myths; for students to learn how to use mapping tools efficiently
Situation	Students plot different destination points as they explore different myths and learn about the cultural significances surrounding the myths.

With visual literacies, this isn't any different. One common skill I continue to be disappointed with is the difficulties students have reading maps and how they continue to be more and more disconnected with these visual tools; of course, I do not fault the teachers who use maps in their classrooms. It simply seems to be more and more reliance on GPS systems. Though GPS devices are reliable and have proven very helpful, students should still know the basic ideas behind reading a map.

When the seventh graders participate in my myth unit (Table 7.4), which is discussed in chapter 4, I post a huge world map on one of my walls. Throughout the unit as we visit different cultures through the myths we read, I put pushpins in the poster of the places we have visited.

One activity I have the students participate in is using the mapping tools on Google Maps and MapQuest. While having the option of using one of these tools, the students complete research where they answer a series of questions for their travelogue given to them by the Social Studies teacher and myself. The students answer the list of questions after we visit a new country and then they answer a few overall questions about their trip through the different countries. The final question is only answered at the end of the unit. Figure 7.1 shows an example of a seventh grader's travelogue.

1. What is the total distance we have traveled on our myth adventure?
2. What other countries have we visited as we have traveled from country to country?
3. Are any of the countries that we have traveled through along the way a threat to the country we are visiting for our myth?
4. What similarities and differences do you see between the countries we have visited?

5. How have these countries changed over time? How have they stayed the same?
6. What geographic landforms surrounding the country or in the country could have helped in creating a myth we have read about?
7. What are your thoughts on how we have done our myth unit? Positives? Negatives? Are there ways Mr. Hyler can improve it?

I require my students to print a map (Image 7.4) when we near the end of our myth unit with all of the countries we have visited while reading our myths, which totals five. Also, the students are required to embed this map into a Google Document where they have answered the questions given above. They share their document with me when it is time to turn it in.

Myth Travelogue

Greece to France

1. So far we have traveled about 721 miles or 1160 Kilometers (www.distancefromto.net/) from Greece to Turkey.
2. We have not visited any other country as we left Greece. Turkey is directly east of Greece.
3. There are not any countries between Greece and France. It is interesting to know that these two countries do get along with each other but have fought against each other in four major wars. The Greco-Turkish War (1897), the First Balkan War of 1912 to 1913, World War I (1914 to 1918) and finally the Turkish War of Independence. (wikipedia.com)
4. When it comes to the topic of food, there are some things they eat that are the same, but they just have different names. For examples, Gyros are present in both countries. Both countries eat a lot of lamb too. Turkish people drink a lot of coffee unlike the people who live in Greece. There are different languages spoken in each country.

    The climate is basically the same for both countries because they are in the same region. Turkey seems to have higher elevation than Greece.

5. Greece is going through economic hardships right now and a possible economic collapse. Turkey is in the middle of what seems to be a revolution. Both countries have embraced the traditions celebrated from their early existence.
6. Both countries are mountainous. Greece has a lot more mountains that divide the country up. In terms of higher elevations and the mountains, I can see how Greece could use Zeus to explain lightning and his wrath he may cast when the people were being bad.
7. Question #7 will be answered at the end of our travel log.

Figure 7.1 Myth Travelogue Assignment

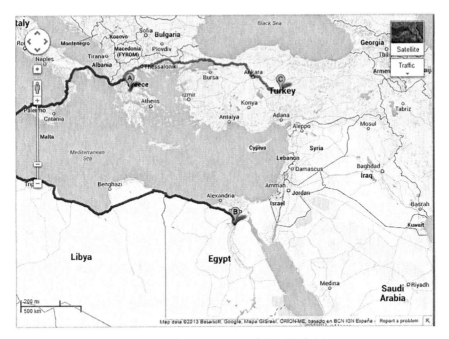

Image 7.4 Screencapture of Our Myth Map

The students enjoy this approach because they are learning most of the information themselves. A lot of this unit is inquiry, which requires the students to do research to find the information they need to answer the questions. As a class, we spend time discussing the myths we read, but the answers to their travelogue questions are not directly discussed in class. The students keep all of their information in Evernote (chapter 5) or in a Google Doc where they can revisit their research when they are answering the questions. While the students are working on this, I give them benchmarks to reach as they we go through the unit so they are not waiting until the end of the unit to do all of the work. By having my students do a small inquiry project, I am better preparing them for the bigger multigenre project they will complete in late spring.

Developing Infographics

In terms of graphs and charts, I feel these types of visual literacies can be taught incorrectly. I don't say this to be insulting; I say it having reflected on my own experiences with different classes of students. My first thoughts about graphs and charts go back to my first few years of teaching; my belief then was

Table 7.5 MAPS for Report and Infographic

Mode	Year-long project and written report (salmon project)
Media	Graphs, charts
Audience	Peers, teachers, Department of Environmental Quality (DEQ) officials, Department of Natural Resources (DNR) officials
Purpose	Show predator/prey relationships at the creek; help determine if release site is sufficient enough to release the salmon
Situation	Creation of a written report that includes visuals and is completed on Google Docs; assignment handed in via Dropbox

that you saw a majority of graphs and charts only in science and math. Since those first few years, I have learned that graphs not only go beyond curricular boundaries, but students need to see graphs beyond simply being able to construct them out of the data they gather and the simplistic questions associated with interpreting graphs. Students should be able to look multiple graphs and make appropriate evaluations of them; comparing the information that the graphs are displaying or asking a more rigorous question help students do this. For example, what do the graphs not tell us?

Also, when my students were examining different types of graphs prior to them completing their Salmon in the Classroom project reports (a project sponsored by our Department of Natural Resources where students raise and release salmon), they were looking at graphs that displayed vacation destinations people have in our state. After the initial discussion of the data from the graph, I wanted to extend my students' thinking so I asked the question, "What does the data tell the tourist division of our state department?" This question can't be answered from the graph but instead requires the student to look at all of the information as a whole and make appropriate determinations based on the graph. I feel as an educator we need to get out of the rut of just teaching students how to simply read a date or a percentage from a graph and chart. Furthermore, we as teachers need to challenge our students to think broader in terms of how we can require our students to display information in their writing besides placing a traditional bar graph within their writing. We should challenge our students to look at other visuals they can place within their writing, such as an infographic.

In terms of constructing a graph, I enjoy having my students use Infogr.am, a simple application for making infographics (http://infogr.am). Infographics use a specific context while presenting data in a graphic form. In other words, you can plug information from a spreadsheet and choose to display data in a pie chart, line graph, scatter plot, and so on (see MAPS in Table 7.5). Users can create interactive infographics and charts with just a few simple clicks and can not only save and post what has been created but also embed it into Web sites. Additionally, the basic features are free, but you can get more options to choose from if you upgrade to the pro version. Sign-up requires an e-mail address or the user can link it to an existing Facebook or Twitter account.

Specifically, the tool allows the user to use text, pictures, and various graphs (line, bar, scatterplot, pictorial, pie, etc.) to display different types of information. Image 7.6 is a simple infographic that was created during the salmon project. This student looked at a sample of 100 fish from the creek where the salmon were going to be released and broke down how many different species were present at the time of the sample.

As mentioned earlier, the infographic that you make is interactive. Anyone looking at the graph can hover a mouse over each part and see the percentage of the population each type of fish comprises. If the user hovers over the name of a fish that is present in the graph, the user can see where it is located in the graph.

	A	B	C	D	E	F	G	H	I
1	Type of Fish	2013							
2	White Sucker	48							
3	Brown Trout	3							
4	Northern Pike	6							
5	Northern Hog Sucker	4							
6	Central Mud Minnow	3							
7	Large Mouth Bass	2							
8	Johnny Darter	4							
9	Common Shiner	12							
10	Creek Chub	7							
11	Blackside Darter	3							
12	Blacknose Dace	8							

Image 7.5 Student Data from the Salmon Project

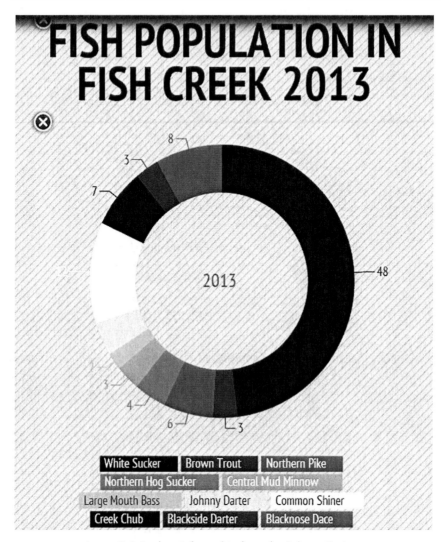

FISH POPULATION IN FISH CREEK 2013

2013

8
3
7
48
3
4
6
3

White Sucker | Brown Trout | Northern Pike
Northern Hog Sucker | Central Mud Minnow
Large Mouth Bass | Johnny Darter | Common Shiner
Creek Chub | Blackside Darter | Blacknose Dace

Image 7.6 Student Infographic from the Salmon Project

Students enjoy the different options they have for graphs and how they can add their own touches such as a picture or even a map. For the salmon project, some students plugged in a map to show where the salmon were released. One other great feature about Infogr.am is the user can import information from a spreadsheet instead of recreating the data on the graph. The data can be imported from Excel, Google Drive, or other CSV files.

Image 7.5 shows what the spreadsheet looks like in Infogr.am. You can see how simple it was for the student to produce the graph for Fish Creek (Image 7.6) using the data from the spreadsheet.

Using infographics, graphs, and charts enhances reports, papers, and projects. Students are not only appealing to visuals learners, but they are incorporating creativity into their reports. So, not only will their reports be more creativity appealing, but also appealing infographics help readers to analyze and think more critically about the material presented.

Final Thoughts

It wasn't until three years ago that I really began to look strongly at how visual literacies impact my learners and the way I teach my students. Being in a visual world and culture only enhances and gives more meaning to what I try to get across to my students. Students need to think more critically when it comes to composing or using visuals. Too many times students use the excuse something is "cool" instead of thinking hard about what effect it is going to have on their audience and how it can enhance their written word. Challenging students to continually familiarize themselves with not only visual literacies, but also narrative, informational, and argumentative writing can seem overwhelming. Still, there are ways to meet all these goals. Our next chapter delves into the idea of using the multigenre research project to help students get more and more familiar with these genres.

Our Many Voices (Multigenre Research Project)

At its core, multigenre means letting go—letting writers decide.

(Kittle, 2008, p. 163)

The Common Core State Standards caught my attention almost immediately when I saw the wording research *project* instead of research *paper*. Because I already did a research project with my students, I felt I was already ahead in terms of implementing the CCSS.

I am not going to lie; I dislike the term *research paper*. From the time I was in high school and all the way through college, my passion for writing an expository research paper never increased an ounce. When I finally thought I was done with the disengagement that accompanies research papers, I learned that as a teacher that my students were going to have to complete a research paper. Needless to say, I was not looking forward to the countless hours I was going to spend reading expository papers that were five to six pages long and the gallons of coffee I might consume.

I was in desperate search an alternative. In 2007, I attended a one-day professional development conference on writing. My goal for any PD I attend is to take one thing back to my classroom I can use. In this particular case, I tucked the multigenre research project into my tool belt. It seemed I had found my solution.

Regarding the multigenre project, I was enticed by the idea of students exploring many genres of writing while focusing on one topic. Tom Romano, who is known quite well for his work with multigenre, discussed his views on the topic in *Teaching the Neglected "R": Rethinking Writing Instruction in Secondary Classrooms* (2007). "I don't want student to become Johnny-One-Genres, which is what I was until I got to college . . . I oppose such exclusivity.

Writing is a big world mural, not a snapshot" (Romano, 2007, pp. 88–89). Romano goes on to explain how multigenre allows for multiple voices from the students as well as the use of their imagination.

> W.7.7–Conduct short research projects to answer a question, drawing on several sources and generating additional related, focused questions for further research and investigation.

In addition to changing my approach from a single expository paper to students writing in many genres, I began to realize upon the release of the CCSS that I was already incorporating one of the many rigorous standards that has been set forth. For instance, writing standard 7.7 fully supports how I approach research in my class. Also, because the CCSS focuses on informational, argument, and narrative writing, I can require my students to include a piece from each of the main genres in their mulitgenre research project. I have found this approach to work both with my students, who want to be engaged and interested, as well as with the curricular approach to genre study that many scholars advocate (Dean, 2008; Fleischer & Andrew-Vaughan, 2009; Lattimer, 2003). The Writing Now report, for instance, demonstrates the need for students to write in varied contexts for a variety of real-world audiences (National Council of Teachers of English, 2008).

Furthermore, I found the idea of the project more rewarding for middle school students because it gives them choice, not only of their topic for research but also of the genres that they would explore throughout the project. Also, it allows them to tap into their creative side, so there is the potential for me to hear different voices within the different pieces of writing they compose. Because we have had some experience in each of these genres by the time we get to this project (chapters 3, 4, and 5), my students are fairly comfortable with them. For any genre the students are introduced to that they may not be familiar with, I give a short mini-lesson on during which I show multiple examples for the students to use as models. Some students may approach me asking about a genre not discussed in class; I address those inquiries on an individual basis and help the student decide if it will be a good fit with his or her topic and the question(s) he or she is trying to answer.

When I began my quest for implementing the multigenre project in my classroom, I started with Camille Allen's *The Multigenre Research Paper: Voice, Passion, and Discovery in Grades 4–6* (2001). At that time I was teaching sixth grade, so it was an appropriate text for my situation. In the beginning chapter, Allen echoes the same thoughts I have had pertaining to the multigenre research project:

> I've seen multigenre research papers change students' negative perceptions of research, writing, and oral presentations. When given the chance to select their own topics to research, decide which genres to write in, and determine how they want to present their findings to an audience, students change. They become empowered. They assume ownership of their learning and display pride in showing off their accomplishments. They grow. (Allen, 2001, p. 1)

Choice, empowerment, pride, and growth are excellent ways to describe what happens with the multigenre project. Middle school students thrive when they have choices, helping them to take ownership of their learning. The multigenre project brings a whole new level to the world of research when students feel they have a say in the learning process and they feel pride in their work; this leads to academic growth in the student. Now I am more engaged as their teacher when I read through my students' research projects; I see a culmination of creativity, hard work, and learned knowledge.

And in terms of knowledge, my students get a chance to broaden their writing horizons. Students get the chance to "play" with conventions within the different genres. Melinda Putz argues that

> the multigenre project allows a great deal of freedom too. Yet, certainly it does not do away with convention; it just widens the parameters. That may mean writing labyrinthine sentences or fragments, using capital letters within words or purposeful misspellings—whatever it takes to communicate the ideas and the mood inherent to the subject. (2006, p. 3)

Students are constantly exploring the different ways language is used through grammar lessons, writing assignments, and the study of author's craft (or the manner in which the author uses literary devices and narrative elements). The multigenre project allows students to experiment and implement different uses of language and explore the effect it can have.

As a language arts teacher, with this project, I am graced with the opportunity to see how much my students grow as writers while, at the same time, they

Table 8.1 Timeline for the Multigenre Research Project

Week One	Week Two	Weeks Three and Four
• Exploring the question, What is research? • Identifying good sources • Developing a smart question • Evaluating the credibility of the Dihydrogen Monoxide Web site	• Generating list of potential topics • Refining and narrowing topics • Rationalizing topic choices	• Gathering, organizing, and citing sources • Conferring with students about their topic and the research process
Week Five	**Week Six**	**Ongoing Teachable Moments**
• Exploring various genres • Aligning research with how students can present their findings with the genres • Developing individual pieces of project • Participating in peer response groups	• Finishing genres and overall projects • Completing works cited page • Presenting projects in gallery walk • Reflecting on the research process and what was completed	• Determining the specifics of MLA formatting • Modeling of different genres to help with effectively displaying research • Teaching conventions through conferring and mini-lessons

are learning how to be effective researchers. Before going into lots of detail about the entire project, Table 8.1 is a quick overview of the lessons I teach my seventh graders over the course of six weeks, all of which will be explained in more detail throughout the chapter.

Multigenre and Choosing Topics

When I first start to describe the multigenre research project to my students, they have a lot of questions. It is necessary to take time to answer the questions and provide an appropriate explanation of the project. I generally start the discussion with a short explanation and show my former students' projects. For example, I often show a "glog," or digital poster, that a student composed two years ago using Eminem as his topic. The student used multiple visual literacies, audio, video, and text within in his glog.

Multigenre projects take time. Oftentimes, it can take four weeks, or perhaps longer. If my seventh graders are doing the project, it takes about six weeks. In the past, I have done an abbreviated version of the project that takes no longer than three weeks; however, the quality of research the students do can be compromised if not planned out carefully.

During the initial stages of the project I do not show the students their rubric, despite the advice that some educational researchers give about sharing the rubric first. Instead, I share the rubric with the students after they have chosen their topic, which is within the first week of the project. I want them to focus on two areas at this time, not just a rubric. First, I want them to think about their topic. I have them open the Google Doc they have created for journal writing. I ask the students to make a list of topics that they have always wanted to know more about. I tell them to limit their list to three to five topics because I don't want them to feel overwhelmed when it comes time to make a choice on a topic. As with any other time I give students a choice on topics, I get a handful of students who say, "I can't think of anything Mr. Hyler!" When this happens, I tell them they are in luck because I have generated a list of potential topics for them. You can find the complete list on our resource wiki: createcomposeconnect.wikispace.com. Table 8.2 shows a few examples from that list. Romano and Allen both offer a list of topics in their books, but I suggest compiling your own list so it can relate better to the students. My list is comprised of popular trends that students are familiar with; I also incorporate topics from social studies, math, and science on which I believe my students may want more information.

I never think that my students are going to be experts in the topic they choose. But in fact, they themselves may think that they are indeed experts;

Table 8.2 Topics Generated During the 2012–2013 School Year

People	Events/Ideas
Justin Bieber	9/11
One Direction	The war in Afghanistan
Abraham Lincoln	Gettysburg
Jefferson Davis	Salmon
George Washington	Pythagorean theorem
Osama Bin Laden	Michigan, our great state
Barack Obama	Computers
Suzanne Collins	Cell phones
Gary Paulsen	Text messaging
Lebron James	FOIL (math concept)
Kobe Bryant	American Revolution

however, this project is about inquiry. Even if a student thinks he or she knows everything about Lebron James, for instance, he or she should compose a list of questions about James and spend time investigating multiple resources, digital or physical.

The second main point to keep in mind as students choose their topic is that some may need help narrowing their topics down. For instance, my student Luke chose pizza for his topic. When I sat him down to talk one on one, I explained to him that pizza is a huge topic. I asked him what specifically he wanted to know about pizza. For example, I asked him if he was interested in the origins of pizza or if he was interested in how pizza chains such as Pizza Hut got started. He wrote down some notes, and from there he formulated his three questions:

1. Where was the first pizza made, and what were the ingredients?
2. What is the biggest and most expensive pizza on record?
3. Who came up with idea of delivering pizza, and when did delivery first start?

Students form these questions because I want them to have a focus when it comes to researching their topic. When I talk to my students I encourage them to be as specific as possible. I want them to get more specific with individual people, brands, or products. Students should be asking multiple questions and have passion for their topic. We discuss asking who, what, where, when, why, and how. The questions will be their guide during the research process, which is where they will use various technologies. One of those pieces of technology students could be using is the "multigenre mapper" tool offered by the Read, Write, Think Web site (readwritethink.org). Find a direct link to this resource on our wiki page for chapter 8.

The multigenre mapper is an interactive tool that students can use to create multimodal work. There are three different sections labeled A, B, and C where the student can place the different genres of writing they have created, helping the students better organize how they present their research. The student creates one drawing and three written sections. The student can plan out what he or she is going to do before using the interactive tool by completing the planning sheet that accompanies the tool. You can find the link to the planning sheet on our resource site. I feel it would work well at the elementary level, too. It is an easy tool for students to use, and it helps them to think about their topic and the different genres they want to explore.

As the students are thinking about their topic and questions, I continue to dig deeper with them. I ask them to answer the question of why they are choosing their particular topic. I want my students to have a purpose as well as a focus when it comes to doing research. I don't accept answers along the lines of "Because I like it." There needs to be a reason why students chose certain topics. Sometimes it is a potential career option; other times, a future hobby. Also, students may just find the topic interesting; it's something they have always wanted to know more about. Below are a few responses my students have given me:

- Pizza: I chose this topic because it's a chance to learn about something that we all like. Then when I see pizza, I can tell people what I know.

- Off-road racing: I chose it because my grandpa used to race, and I want to know more about it.

- Bubble gum: it seems interesting to know who came up with something you can chew on that tastes good and why it was created.

Please fill out the survey by the end of class on Wednesday, May 15.

What topic(s) are you thinking about for research?

What questions do you want answered about your topic? (In other words, what are you hoping to learn about your topic?)
List at least 3 fundamental questions you have about your topic

Why did you choose this topic?
Please think about this questions. Please don't say because I like it!

List at least 5 sources where you found information
For example, write down the URL (www.whatever.com)

What other genre besides the 1 page written report are you thinking of doing?
It can be digital. For example, a video, voice recording, etc. Explain in detail what you are doing.

What is your name?
First and Last please

Image 8.1 Google Survey for Multigenre Topics

Of course I do get a few students who don't put a lot of effort into their reason why. I conference with these students and require them to be more critical about why they are choosing their topic. If you are wondering how I collect all the information from my students, know that I use Google Forms to essentially give my students a survey (see a link on our wiki page to a sample). The information from the survey automatically gets put into a spreadsheet, and I can revisit the spreadsheet when I have conversations with my students about what they are doing in terms of research and the project; it is beneficial to have conversations with my students so they can process what we have done. A sample survey is shown in Image 8.1.

Furthermore, it is beneficial to give the students a deadline for when they *can't* change their topic. Every year I get a handful of students that approach me and want to change their topic, usually two weeks into the project. I give students the topic deadline so they can stay on task, and I feel it provides them a well needed challenge, especially for the students who sometimes give up easily when they proclaim they can't find any information on their topic. As most of us have experienced, this generally happens because they have lost interest. I simply try to avoid this problem.

Researching

Researching anything is more than typing a few words in the text box on Google or Yahoo. It takes time and energy, and it is important to know if the information provided has come from a reliable source. Researching can be exhausting, and it is not any secret that students don't want to spend quality time researching their topic. I had my students take a poll, and 95% of them use Google to not only find information about their topic but also to answer questions they have about various topics. Using Google is just a start; teaching students to research effectively is the most important aspect of the research project.

Barry Lane discusses this idea further: "When you research any subject, pay particular attention to the facts that take you by surprise—the ones that make you turn to yourself and say, 'I never knew that'" (2003, p. 24). Researching should be more than just "looking up" information on a topic. It should be a learning process as well as engaging for the student. There are multiple facets about conducting research that I address in my classroom such as Web site credibility, understanding (and using) Wikipedia, using library databases, and organizing and citing information. I'll share my thoughts on each one of these below.

Web Site Credibility

Oftentimes students will click on the first Web site Google provides and won't investigate further. Because students need to understand Web site evaluation as a component of their research process (and as a life skill in the twenty-first century), I start by showing them a Web site about Dihydrogen Monoxide (www.dhmo.org/facts.html). For those of you not familiar with the substance, it is just water (H_2O or DHMO)! But my students don't usually know that right away. When talking to the students about reliable Internet resources, I feel the Dihydrogen Monoxide Web site is the best example to show them the deceptive information people can put on the Internet.

Though the site does provide truthful facts, it is the perspective that the author takes in delivering the information to their audience that is misleading. For instance, the Web site states that DHMO is found in numerous poisonous substances such as sulfuric acid. Though this is true, it doesn't deem water a substance we have to ban from existence. I am always humored by my middle school students' reactions to this Web site, especially when they look at some of the dangers of dealing with Dihydrogen Monoxide. I had a student want to start a petition in the school to ban the substance before she even knew what it was. When I do reveal to the students what DHMO is, their reactions range from disbelief to wanting to reread the information. Others shake their heads and want me to go to other Web sites to further investigate. When students ask me to look at other Web sites, I get excited because it shows that students understand that they should look to multiple sources to verify information.

Understanding and Using Wikipedia

Wikipedia is a great site to use to teach students about investigating further into whether or not information is reliable and posted by credible individuals. Furthermore, it is a place where students can expand their searches if they are having difficulty finding multiple sources about their topic. Most educators may be cringing at the thought of me using Wikipedia, but I assure you my students become better researchers by the end of this project. At the bottom of most Wikipedia entries, there are usually both reference sections and an external links section. These sections are the most valuable to me and my students. Why?

References

1. ^ Miller, Hanna (April/May 2006). "American Pie" ⟐. American Heritage Magazine. Retrieved 4 May 2012

2. ^ Linda Civitello (2007). Cuisine and culture: a history of food and people ⟐ (Paperback ed.). Wiley. p. 98. ISBN 0-471-74172-8.

3. ^ Via the Judaeo-Spanish pita. Though the Hebrew word pitāh is spelled like the Aramaic pittedā/pittā, which is related to Levantine Arabic fatten, they are not connected historically. Oxford English Dictionary, 3rd edition, April 2009 s.v. 'pita'

4. ^ "Pizza Margherita History and Recipe" ⟐. Italy Magazine. 14 March 2011. Retrieved 23 April 2012.

5. ^ "Was margherita pizza really named after Italy's queen?" ⟐. BBC Food. 28 December 2012. Retrieved 31 December 2012.

6. ^ Brainbridge, Sophie; Glynn, Joanne (2005). Food of Italy ⟐. Murdoch Books. p. 167. ISBN 1740454642

7. ^ "Selezione geografica ⟐. Europa eu.int. 2009-02-23. Retrieved 2009-04-02.

8. ^ "Associazione Vera Pizza Napoletana" ⟐. Pizzanapoletana.org. Retrieved 2012-07-07.

9. ^ "Vera Pizza Napoletana Specification | Verace Pizza Napoletana ⟐. Fornobravo.com 2004-05-24. Retrieved 2009-04-02.

10. ^ Naples pizza makers celebrate EU trademark status ⟐. BBC News. 4 February 2010

11. ^ "Publication of an application pursuant to Article 8(2) of Council Regulation (EC) No 509/2006 on agricultural products and foodstuffs as traditional specialties guaranteed – Pizza napoletana (2008/C 40/08)" ⟐. OJEU. 14 February 2009

12. ^ Adam Kuban (2008-09-12). "What Is Grandma Pizza? Erica Marcus Explains Once More | Slice Pizza Blog" ⟐. Slice.seriouseats.com. Retrieved 2012-07-07.

13. ^ "Bill for traditional Italian pizza" ⟐. Senato it. Retrieved 2009-04-02

14. ^ "Permissible ingredients and methods of processing" ⟐. Senato it. Retrieved 2009-04-02.

15. ^ EU grants Neapolitan pizza Traditional Specialty Guaranteed label ⟐. Pizza Marketplace

16. ^ Svenska dagbladet Pizza statistics according to AC Nielsen

17. ^ "Additions to the Australian lexicographical record" ⟐

18. ^ "Capital da pizza: sabores para todos / 2007-07-10 00:18:29 – 163164631 / Gazeta Mercantil ⟐. Indexet.gazetamercantil.com.br. Retrieved 2009-04-02.

19. ^ "Smokin Joes Pizza » About Us" ⟐. Smokinjoespizza.com. 1993-07-21. Retrieved 2012-07-07.

20. ^ Restaurants in Israel – Search results for restaurants in Jerusalem ⟐

21. ^ Klingbail, Sivan (2005-05-03). "Pizza Hut revamps to survive" ⟐. Haaretz.com. Retrieved 2012-07-07.

22. ^ Ceccarini R. (2010) Food Workers as Individual Agents of Culinary Globalization. Pizza and Pizza Chefs in Japan. Sophia University. Tokyo.

23. ^ Ceccarini R. (2011) Pizza and Pizza Chefs in Japan: A Case of Culinary Globalization. Brill Publishers. Netherlands. http://www.brill.nl/pizza-and-pizza-chefs-japan-case-culinary-

24. ^ "Foreign food franchises (Pakistan) | Franchises from ⟐ AllBusiness.com. Retrieved 2010-02-19.

25. ^ Paul, Jean. "Advertising, Marketing, Media, Digital, PR News and more – Campaign Asia-Pacific ⟐. Media.asia. Retrieved 2012-07-07.

26. ^ "First North Korean pizzeria opens" ⟐. BBC News. 2009-03-16. Retrieved 2010-05-22.

27. ^ "Dominos.se (Swedish)" ⟐. Retrieved 2011-07-10.

28. ^ Asimov, Eric (June 10, 1998), "New York Pizza, the Real Thing Makes a Comeback" ⟐, New York Times, retrieved September 24, 2006

29. ^ "Food Standards Agency – Survey of pizzas" ⟐. Food.gov.uk. 2004-07-08. Retrieved 2009-04-02.

30. ^ "Health | Fast food salt levels 'shocking'" ⟐. BBC News. 2007-10-18. Retrieved 2009-04-02.

31. ^ "Mario Negri – Istituto di Ricerche Farmacologiche" ⟐. Marionegri.it 1953-02-01. Retrieved 2009-04-02.

32. ^ "Mama Lena's pizza 'One' for the book.. of records" ⟐. Pittsburghlive.com. Retrieved 2009-04-02.

33. ^ "Chef cooks £2,000 Valentine pizza" ⟐. BBC News. 2007-02-14. Retrieved 2012-07-07.

34. ^ "Brick Oven Cecina" ⟐. Fornobravo.com. Retrieved 2009-04-02.

35. ^ Helga Rosemann. Flammkuchen: Ein Streifzug durch das Land der Flammkuchen mit vielen Rezepten und Anregungen (Offenbach: Höma-Verlag, 2009).

Image 8.2 Reference section on the Wikipedia page for pizza

> W.8.9—Draw evidence from literary or informational texts to support analysis, reflection, and research.

When you look at Image 8.2 you will notice there are 35 references for Luke's topic on pizza. This not only helps Luke to determine if the Wikipedia entry is reliable, but it gives Luke potentially 35 other sources where he can go and locate additional information for his topic. In addition, he can quickly peruse the references and see if the author of the Wikipedia article used reliable sources. For instance, reference 28 is from the *New York Times*, a very dependable resource. Luke can then make a conscious decision as to whether or not he should use this article for his research.

My intention with demonstrating to my students how to do this with Wikipedia is that they will carry over the skills to other Web sites they visit during the research process. Also, it helps to eliminate students from claiming that they are unable to find sources. Finally, our attitudes about Wikipedia— and the crowdsourced, collaborative writing that keeps it up-to-date and accurate—can and should change. For an interesting story about how Wikipedia's community of writers and editors actually compose the entries, have students read the Wikipedia article on maintaining a "neutral point of view."

Using Library Databases

In addition to all the information that can be found through basic Web searches and from links in Wikipedia, there is a whole other "deep web" of information that hides behind password protected databases. In the past my school has paid yearly subscriptions to multiple databases. However, there are many free databases that exist that can give students another resource besides visiting multiple Web sites. One particular database is called MEL (MEL.org) or the Michigan e-Library, which is free to Michigan residents; there they have free access to full articles, books, images, and more. I am not sure if other states offer this same type of resource for their residents, but it is worth investigating if you are not a Michigan resident.

I use databases such as MEL with my students because, as mentioned, they give students a resource other than a Web page. One of the greatest aspects of MEL is that it provides links to other valuable databases. Some of the databases that it links to are not free; regardless, being able to access multiple databases from one place saves time during the research process. In addition to MEL, I steer my students toward ERIC (eric.ed.gov), a database that is sponsored by the United States Department of Education and the Institute of Education Science. It offers abstracts and full articles. My seventh and eighth graders can easily navigate both databases. Databases can be very beneficial for those students who say they can't find anything on their topic. I want my students to have zero excuses when it comes to finding information.

Organizing and Citing Information

As students carry on with their research, they need a space to put the information they have gathered. In the past, I have had my students put all of their information on the notecards. Though writing down the information is critically important, especially because the students need to give the proper credit to the individuals who created the information and sites where the information was found, making notecards is time consuming and the cards can easily be lost.

> W.7.8—Gather relevant information from multiple print and digital sources, using search terms effectively; assess the credibility and accuracy of each source; and quote or paraphrase the data and conclusions of others while avoiding plagiarism and following a standard format for citation.

There are several places where students can house the information they gather. Those teachers who don't want to explore other tools can simply have students put information into a Google Doc or use Evernote (mentioned in chapter 5). However, there are tools available that can make the research process easier for your students. The tool I like is Diigo (www.diigo.com). Diigo basically mimics handwritten notes. Students can highlight information from Web sites. Then they can bookmark the information to make it easily accessible. Students can tag the information for the specific genres they have chosen, or they can tag it under the questions they created earlier. The students can access their information on a computer, a cell phone, or a tablet. Diigo has a toolbar that can be added to your browser for easier bookmarking and highlighting of sources.

The looming question that I feel teachers want to the answer to is what exactly am I asking my students to retrieve, and what are they doing with the information? It is important for students to keep their information organized and ready to use. When students are looking for resources and information online, I have them organize their information by retrieving the following.

- site title
- URL
- title of the article
- date the information was published
- author of the article (if available)
- date the student accessed the article
- highlighted content students retrieved from the article
- interpretation of the content highlighted

When students are entering their information into Diigo, they input all of the necessary information that is required by Diigo, which is the URL, title of the Web site, and a description. Where the description box is located, I require the students to put the highlighted content they retrieved from the Web site and their interpretation of the content. Their information is then saved. An example is shown in Image 8.3.

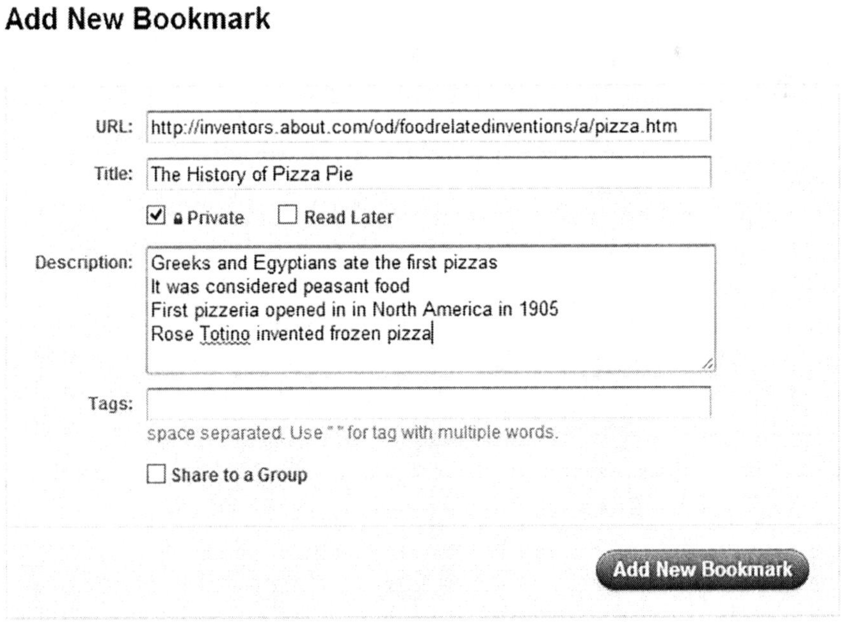

Add New Bookmark

URL: http://inventors.about.com/od/foodrelatedinventions/a/pizza.htm

Title: The History of Pizza Pie

☑ 🔒 Private   ☐ Read Later

Description:
Greeks and Egyptians ate the first pizzas
It was considered peasant food
First pizzeria opened in in North America in 1905
Rose Totino invented frozen pizza

Tags:
space separated. Use " " for tag with multiple words.

☐ Share to a Group

Add New Bookmark

Image 8.3 Input screen for references in Diigo

If Diigo seems too complex, and you are looking for a tool to help guide students to creating just a works cited page, there are resources such as easybib.com and citationmachine.net. Both sites require student to input the required data for a correct citation, and then the site creates the citation for them. Then students can simply cut and paste the citation into a Word document or a Google Doc. Both online tools are easy for students to use and easy for teachers to explain.

Choosing Genres

Think with me for a moment about how the students feel about research papers. Are students genuinely excited about regurgitating facts they have spent hours gathering? Barry Lane brings this very thought to light as he refers to term papers as "terminal" papers and that "they can lose their spark" (2003, p. 13). His wacky we-search book focuses on the idea of reporting the facts in different genres, similar to what Romano refers to in his books. For example, a student completes their research on the Titanic and is ready to report on his or her findings. Instead of typing a five-page report that simply states facts, how about writing a letter from the point of view of one of the passengers as the ship is sinking? The facts become more interesting because now the student has a specific focus when it comes to the actual research. The facts they are trying to find should not only relate to their topic and the three questions they have posed, but the facts should be appropriate for the genres they have chosen. Each student needs to make decisions about what information fits best with each genre.

Choosing the genres is really exciting for the students. I start off by sharing with them a link on Google Drive to a list of genres (Table 8.3). It is also worth noting that the template gallery for Google Docs, as well as that in standard word processing programs, has numerous examples of genres (such as business cards, flyers, brochures, and newsletters) that students could explore (go to https://drive.google.com/templates#).

When thinking through implementing the multigenre project, it is important to consider how many genres you want your students to explore. Remember, if you are looking at a four-week project, you want to allow some time for students to work and ask any questions they may have during the drafting process. I ask my students to choose four genres.

When considering the different genres to help display the information they have learned, it is important to keep two things in mind. First, give students genres they are already familiar with. Next, students will approach you

Table 8.3 Potential Genres for Students to Choose From

Narrative	**Informational**
• Short story • Letter • E-mail • Myth • Diary entry • Poem • Mystery	• Brochures • Interviews • Magazine articles • Newspaper articles • Resume • Eulogy • Manual • Recipe
Argument	**Visual Media**
• Editorials • Commercials • Book review • Advice columns • Campaign speech • Argument essay • Proposal	• Posters (Glogster) • Charts • Maps • Comic strip (Toondoo, Bitstrips, Goanimate) • Timeline • Graphs • Collage • Prezi

about exploring a genre that may not be on your list. I always try to have a list of generic requirements for when this occurs. I often get a handful of students who want to explore a new Web site where they can create their project. However, depending on the genre they want to explore, it may come down to me sitting down with the student and having a one-on-one discussion about the genre he or she is considering.

In terms of thinking about specific genres, I ask the students to consider the three broader genres the CCSS asks us to cover and, in addition, any visual literacies (chapter 7) they could implement into their project. Underneath each genre I give them a list of specific genre pieces. They have either written read text in most of the listed genres, or they are at least aware of the characteristics of the genres. I do spend some time going over each one and providing examples where I can so students not only have a visual, but they also have a student example.

I not only want my students to do well, but I also want them to enjoy what they are doing. Yes, I want my students to have fun! Creating genuine excitement among students can be rather difficult if all they see when you give them a genre list is more writing. Be prepared; your students may turn on you! I use as my two big selling points (1) choice and (2) the simple fact they don't have to complete a massive research paper. So, to counter the potential of a vicious attack from them, I bring to their attention the idea of multimedia. For instance, students don't have to turn in four physical pieces; they can complete a Prezi, a glog, an online comic strip, or a graph. Since beginning this type of project in my class, I have students approach me about completing a poster and I tell them no! I want my students to think outside the box here in terms of the genres they choose. It is too easy to grab a poster, apply some glue, cut out some pictures, and be done. I am not interested in implementing what Mike Schmoker calls a "Crayola Curriculum" (2001). Instead, I want to encourage my students to complete something that is going to make them think and answer the ultimate question I ask all the time in my classroom: Why? Besides, a pile of plain posters is not something I want to lug home and grade.

Putting It All Together

As you can see, with any research, it takes time for the students to get to the point where they are writing. As I mentioned earlier in the chapter, students are going to become self-proclaimed experts in a four to six week stretch. They are going to make mistakes along the way. However, when students finally reach the point when they can create, compose, and connect with their writing, it is well worth the effort and energy put in along the way.

When students are ready to start creating their projects, I double check with each student that they are organized by having a quick one to two minute meeting. The meeting is nothing more than me sitting next to the student and having them show me the information they have gathered and listening to what their plan is for completing their project. As the students get started with their projects I feel it is essential to remind them that they can't just create randomly. Again, it is crucial they tie the work back to the questions they have about their topic and the topic itself.

Because I try to keep my classroom as paperless as possible and I don't want to fill the trunk of my car with an overwhelming amount of student projects, I have students submit their projects through their wiki page. The wiki page that has been created for each student allows them to type directly on the page and make links to Google and Word documents or Web sites.

Wikispaces (www.wikispaces.com) is very user friendly and is easy to sign up for; all you need is a user name and password. Security is never an issue either. You can make it as private or public as you want. As the administrator of the site you have control over who can be a part of this collaborative space. So, as the administrator, you are required to approve each member who requests to join.

Acrostic Poem. . .
Wolves howl to communicate.
Originated in North America, some say.
Loud when howling.
Very pretty.
Eurasion wolf is one kind, and
Steppe is another.

Animoto Video

Image 8.4 Anna's wolf acrostic poem. Photograph from http://www.sxc.hu/

I have also had middle school writing camp participants use a wiki. Although the campers do an abbreviated project, I feel their most recent examples can help show what I want students to do. Anna's example (Image 8.4) shows the use of an acrostic poem, and she created an Animoto video as well, which is her informational piece. The wikispace where the campers posted their work is public, so anyone can see their work. Find the link on our chapter 8 wiki page: createcomposeconnect.wikispaces.com

More Genre Examples

A paperless classroom is a wonderful concept, and I embrace it wholeheartedly. On the other hand, I still need to accommodate students who may want to turn in physical projects. This may occur when students don't have outside access to computers where they can spend extra time working online. So, those students utilize the resources they have such as markers, construction paper, and glue sticks. Again, not my idea of the greatest way to create projects, but I have to meet the needs of those particular students.

Fortunately I have seen some well thought out pieces. The two projects in Images 8.5 and 8.6 are from three years ago. Image 8.5 is a postcard

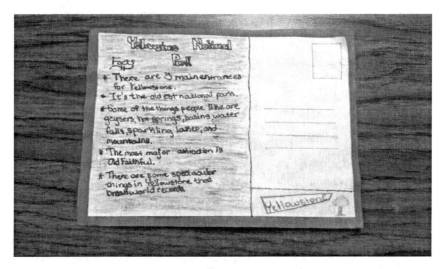

Image 8.5 Yellowstone postcard

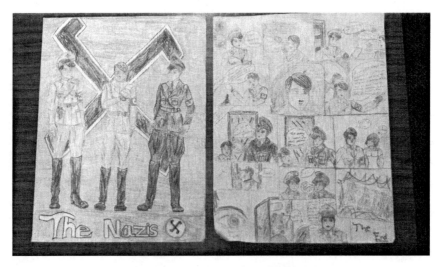

Image 8.6 Comic book about Adolf Hitler

created using construction paper, colored pencils, and markers. The student did his project on Yellowstone National Park. The postcard lists facts about the park to the questions the student developed. Image 8.6 is a comic book on the topic of Adolf Hitler. The young lady who completed this project wanted to know more about Hitler and the regime he created. The comic

Image 8.7 Travis Pastrana baseball card front (Image blurred due to copyright restrictions)

Image 8.8 Travis Pastrana baseball card back (Image blurred due to copyright restrictions)

book she created teaches the reader how the regime was started. These are two student examples well worth holding on to for future students to have as models.

The next two examples are connected to the same student and topic. Being that I teach in a rural school district, I get plenty of students who want research topics connected to hunting, fishing, and other outdoor activities. The student examples below are no exception. The student was heavy into dirt bike racing and riding other off road vehicles. He chose to research a famous dirt bike racer named Travis Pastrana. He focused on a timeline of how Pastrana became one of the best dirt bike riders in the United States—his awards and accomplishments and the specific injuries that he endured through his riding career.

Image 8.9 Travis Pastrana brochure front (Image blurred due to copyright restrictions)

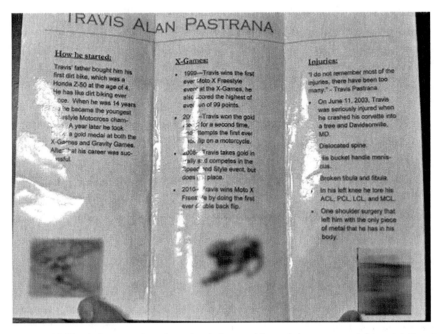

Image 8.10 Travis Pastrana brochure back (Image blurred due to copyright restrictions)

Images 8.7 and 8.8 show the front and back of a baseball card the student created using card stock, Google Docs, a color printer, and the school's laminating machine. Once the student completes a piece underneath each of the general genre headings (argumentative, informational, visual, and narrative) their fifth piece they write can be a genre of their choice. The baseball card falls is informational because of the information the student gave on the back the baseball card.

The student also chose to complete a brochure (Images 8.9 and 8.10) for his fifth genre, another informational piece. He divided the front into three sections, each one addressing his focus questions; on the back, he included additional information. He also had the brochure laminated. Websites such as mybrochuremaker.com are easy to sign up for and use, and they're free. I could have had the student hand this in as a digital file, but I felt it would lose its effect as a brochure if he didn't print it out.

I am always really impressed with how hard the students work on their pieces. Also, I can never get over the creativity of the students.

To better display the work they created, I have my students participate in a gallery walk. A gallery walk is where students can show off their work to classmates, parents, teachers, and principals. Gallery walks can be set up in many different ways. I take two days and divide each class into two groups of about 10 students each. Parents can be invited in during this class time, or you can make a separate time for them come in and view student work. Students set up their computers and any other physical pieces they may have, and the other students walk around and view their classmates' work. The students showing their work discuss the topic they chose and why they chose their particular genres. I instruct the students to not just sit there and say, "Here is my project." I want the students to be engaged with each other. I choose to do this over two days because it takes less time than having all of the students display their work at the same time, and it allows me to have instructional time each day. Overall, the students enjoy the gallery walk.

Assessment and Reflection

At the end of the project, I have the students take some time and reflect back on their experience. As with any writing assignment, I have my students complete a few short questions. I feel students need to think critically about their writing and how they can improve as they continue to grow as writers. With seventh graders I have them answer four questions in their reflection piece.

Questions for reflection (seventh grade)

- What surprised you the most about your topic?

- Was there something you learned or found interesting that you weren't necessarily looking for?

- What challenges did you face along the way during the project?

- Would you have done anything differently with your project?

Figure 8.1 is a reflection from a seventh grader who researched rabbits.

The reflection piece does not have to be anything elaborate. I want it to be enough that the students are going to think about their project and their writing and not just forget about it. Of course, by this point in the year, the students are familiar with the process of reflecting on their writing.

Students shouldn't be the only ones reflecting. I am an educator who is trying to constantly model anything possible to my students. In addition, I want to be a language arts teacher who sets a positive example to my students by reading and writing beside them. It is no different when it comes to reflecting on the lessons and units being taught in my classroom. As far as the multigenre project is concerned, I am constantly trying to find new ways to teach

---

When I did my research on bunnies, I found out some really interesting facts that I did not know before and I was really shocked about some of those things, For example, when I found out that bunnies can purr almost as if like a cat, it really stunned me and made my interest start to ascend! Another thing that really grabbed my attention was that bunnies' ears can get up to 10 cm long or 4 inches long and I really would have never thought that at all so that was really surprising to me. I really enjoyed learning more than I ever had before! Many more things really surprised me, like the fact that bunnies can have up to 28 teeth or more! Although, I found some things that appeared to be rather disappointing to me, such as that bunnies can only live ten years as a pet and that is the most. Most only live 3 or 4 years, which I found really disappointing because I thought they lived much longer. When I did this project I came upon some challenges that made me really struggle. For example, when I did some of my writings, my typing would keep deleting it while I was typing it, which began to make me feel really frustrated and very annoyed. But I kept trying to fix it and later on, it stopped and my writings turned out to be okay. Also, when I tried to put things on my page, they would not go on and I would have to do a lot to get them to stay on and keep them from deleting. But, besides those little things, this turned out to be a really good experience for me and I feel like I have improved so much. But most of all, I enjoyed this marvelous experience very much!

Figure 8.1 Student Reflection on the Multigenre Project

my students about effective research. It is a difficult skill for students to retain, but then again, it is a skill that needs to be practiced not only throughout the year but also year after year. I regularly reexamine how I can deliver productive lessons on research.

Reflecting further, I originally began promoting the use of the multigenre project in my classroom; I saw it as a great unit to encourage boy writers. You can also see some projects on the National Writing Project's Digital Is site (http://digitalis.nwp.org/resource/2737) where I posted information about the multigenre project aimed at teachers who struggle with motivating boy writers. I agree that "[b]oys in school today find themselves whipsawed by several different forces, each of which limits not just what they can write about how also how they can deal with their topics" (Fletcher, 1992, 43). I still say boys benefit from topic and genre choices. However, I can conclude further that boys are not the only ones who benefit by having choice. Girls and boys alike benefit from having the choice and the freedom the multigenre project offers.

Wrapping It Up

Teaching students how to effectively research and write about their research does not have to be a unit we dread. Without a doubt, we must teach students today how to analyze the data that they find and read. Especially with so many digital forms of literacy being thrown at them. It can be difficult for students to process all the information they are bombarded with if they don't have guidance. Without this skill, students never fully understand how to distinguish between quality resources and poor ones. Furthermore, by teaching our students quality research strategies we are helping them to differentiate between fact and opinion. Too many times I see students taking the information they find at face value.

Today, students are finding information via a wide variety of places, such as Web pages, newscasts, instant alerts, or even while at Google Hangout. Now, I know the way I do this unit may not work for every teacher. However, by incorporating the digital component into the unit and allowing students to display what they learned through different media, the students are learning how digital media works. Moreover, they are learning how to effectively reach their audiences while using the different types of digital media. Overall, the project itself lends to students processing and interpreting information better and helps them to understand how multiple employing genres can help others see what they know and have learned.

As with anything you read in this book, our hope is that you find a nugget or two in this chapter that you would like to use in your classroom. The multi-genre research project can be as simple as doing a multigenre mapper or can be very complex; for instance, you could have your students explore up to six different genres and present what they have created in a school gallery walk so others can see what they have been researching. No matter how you integrate this project, the results can be incredible!

Afterword

Through the past eight chapters, you have heard the blended voices of both Troy and me. In this afterword, I have a few final thoughts of my own to share. I honestly feel that if we want to grow as teachers, we need to be open to new ideas and consistently reflect back on what we have done with our students. In my opinion, we only improve as teachers when we take the time to process what has and has not worked in our lessons or units. I think this is true in anything we chose to do as a career. With teaching, if we make the appropriate and necessary changes, we make our students more successful learners.

The way students learn today is significantly different from how students learned 20 years ago. No matter whether or not you support the CCSS, it can't be denied that the CCSS demands that students think critically and requires teachers to implement technology and visuals, as well as student collaboration. In fact, collaboration is an essential skill that is echoed throughout the standards. Whether your particular state is implementing the CCSS or not, there needs to be a shift in our instructional practices if we want our students to be successful in school and in the real world. I would have never realized this myself if it were not for the Chippewa River Writing Project and the summer institute I attended in 2010. It was there where I discovered I needed to make changes in my own approaches I was taking with students when it came to literacy. My hope with coauthoring this book with Troy is to give back to teachers what was given to me at the summer institute: multiple ways to transform my teaching to better reach my students, especially when it comes to collaboration and the effective use of digital tools to meet curricular needs.

Whether my students were reading, writing, collaborating, or enhancing their assignments and projects with the use of technology, I am proud of them and what they accomplished this past school year. However, as I reflect back on what was done, I realize I want to continue to do more. I am constantly striving to make my students more engaged and think critically. For example, earlier in the summer I had the opportunity to attend a summer institute in digital literacy in Rhode Island directed by Renee Hobbs and some other remarkable leaders in the field. I took away many ideas and some amazing new tools I can use in my classroom. I learned that many students don't know how to interpret and analyze online sources correctly, and I also learned that we should always keep the students at the center of our lessons. Also, teaching our students how to purposely use technology means we, as teachers, need to take on some of that responsibility of how to teach them.

Having the privilege to participate in such a remarkable conference in addition to delivering professional development to other educators has allowed me to collaborate with many wonderful individuals. During these conversations I have heard two concerns. First, teachers feel overwhelmed with the amount of digital tools that are available. Second, many teachers feel they don't receive enough time and information in order to effectively use the tools given to them, whether these tools be iPads for their classroom or new software.

To answer the first concern, I encourage teachers to try two new tools a year. That means in 5 years a teacher could be well-versed in 10 different tools. I also encourage teachers to try something outside of their comfort zone. Don't always pick the tool that looks fun or easy. Choose a tool that will help students not only enhance their learning but also bring out their creativity. Our hope in writing this book is that you will be able to find tools that make curricular connections and work in your particular classroom setting.

In terms of teachers not having enough time and information to adequately learn a new tool, I encourage you to play, play, play and to participate in as many professional development opportunities that you can. We need to give ourselves permission to play, explore, fail, and try again. I know, I know, you hear that from Ken Robinson and all the other edu-gurus . . . but you don't have time. Trust me, make the time to play and both you and your students will benefit from it.

Also, talk with your principals and technology directors about having sessions on using new tools. One of the most beneficial professional development sessions I have attended was at the beginning of a school year: my principal had teachers sign up to show each other what digital tools were being used in the classrooms. My point in sharing this is to encourage you to have conversations with your colleagues about what they are using in their classes. Perhaps even teaming up could help those who are reluctant to implement digital tools. Using digital tools and implementing technology can be a positive learning experience for both your students and you.

Teaching and coauthoring a book has been a very rewarding experience. I shared with my students what was happening, and they really did a remarkable job of providing feedback on the lessons I taught them. As I finished my units and lessons this past year, I took to the computer and wrote each chapter, finishing the book this past summer. What was really beneficial to me was the amount of reflecting on my teaching I was able to do while writing the book. As Troy and I talked through and wrote the chapters, we both saw the potential for improvements in what I was doing with lessons and units. With his help, I know next school year's lessons will be that much better. As with any of my lessons I will go back and tweak them to best fit the needs of my students.

Reflecting back on my lessons is just the beginning for me. I want to continue to explore the world of digital literacies and how I can make my students more successful in such a demanding world. I want to take the time to play with the new tool, apps, and handheld devices that continue to emerge. More importantly, I want to continue to help teachers discover how digital literacies can have a significant impact on our students today. Perhaps I will write another book as education continues its shift to digital literacies. Until then, you can follow our continued thinking about digital literacy on our blog: createcomposeconnect.wordpress.com.

I have really enjoyed the work I have done with Troy and the Chippewa River Writing Project. I look forward to leading more professional development sessions, writing, and learning beside teaching colleagues from across the nation.

—Jeremy Hyler, August 2013

References

Allen, C.A. (2001). *The Multigenre Research Paper: Voice, Passion, and Discovery in Grades 4–6*. Portsmouth, NH: Heinemann.

Anderson, J. (2005). *Mechanically Inclined: Building Grammar, Usage, and Style into Writer's Workshop*. Portland, ME: Stenhouse Publishers.

Anderson, J. (2007). *Everyday Editing*. Portland, ME: Stenhouse Publishers.

Anderson, J. (2011). *Ten Things Every Writer Needs to Know*. Portland, ME: Stenhouse Publishers.

Atwell, N. (1998). *In the Middle: New Understandings About Writing, Reading, and Learning* (2nd ed.). Portsmouth, NH: Boynton/Cook.

Bainbridge, K., & Holman, B. (2011). *The Common Core: Clarifying Expectations for Teachers & Students?: English Language Arts Grade 7*. Columbus, OH: McGraw-Hill Education.

Bauerlein, M. (2008). *The Dumbest Generation: How the Digital Age Stupefies Young Americans and Jeopardizes Our Future*. New York: Tarcher.

Benjamin, A., & Berger, J. (2010). *Teaching Grammar: What Really Works*. Larchmont, NY: Eye on Education.

Blume, J. (2007). *Tales of a Fourth Grade Nothing*. New York: Puffin Books.

Burke, J. (2003). *Writing Reminders: Tools, Tips, and Techniques*. Portsmouth, NH: Heinemann.

Burke, J. (2013). *Responding to Student Writing Using Voice Memo*. Retrieved from http://youtube.com/watch?v=6xuSp5-8Bu0&feature=youtube_gdata_player

Burmark, L. (2002). *Visual Literacy: Learn to See, See to Learn*. Alexandria, VA: Association for Supervision and Curriculum Development.

Byrne, R. (2013, March 6). Questions to Ask When Planning Video Projects. *Free Technology for Teachers*. Retrieved from http://freetech4teachers.com/2013/03/questions-to-ask-when-planning-video.html#.Ugzm82SAdqo

Calkins, L. (1994). *The Art of Teaching Writing* (2nd ed.). Portsmouth, NH: Heinemann.

Carr, N. (2008, July 1). Is Google Making Us Stupid? *The Atlantic*. Retrieved from http://www.theatlantic.com/magazine/archive/2008/07/is-google-making-us-stupid/6868/

Cleary, B. (2000). *Dear Mr. Henshaw*. New York: HarperCollins.

Collins, S. (2008). *The Hunger Games*. New York: Scholastic Press.

Collins, S. (2009). *Catching Fire*. New York: Scholastic Press.

Collins, S. (2010). *Mockingjay*. New York: Scholastic Press.

Common Core State Standards Initiative. (2010). Common Core State Standards Initiative. The Standards. English Language Arts Standards. Retrieved from http://corestandards.org/the-standards/english-language-arts-standards

Conley, M.W., Freidhoff, J. R., Sherry, M. B., & Tuckey, S. F. (2008). *Meeting the Challenge of Adolescent Literacy: Research We Have, Research We Need*. New York: Guilford Press.

Consortium for School Networking. (2011, September 13). Acceptable Use Policies in the Web 2.0 and Mobile Era. Retrieved from http://cosn.org/Initiatives/ParticipatoryLearning/Web20MobileAUPGuide/tabid/8139/Default.aspx

Daniels, H. (2002). *Literature Circles: Voice and Choice in Book Clubs and Reading Groups* (2nd ed.). Portland, ME: Stenhouse Publishers.

Dean, D. (2008). *Genre Theory: Teaching, Writing, and Being*. Urbana, IL: National Council of Teachers of English. Retrieved from http://loc.gov/catdir/toc/ecip086/2007050447.html

DeVoss, D., Eidman-Aadahl, E., & Hicks, T. (2010). *Because Digital Writing Matters: Improving Student Writing in Online and Multimedia Environments*. San Francisco, CA: Jossey-Bass.

Drooker, E. (2009). *Blood Song: A Silent Ballad*. Milwaukie, OR: Dark Horse Comics.

Fisher, D., & Frey, N. (2011, February). Academic Language in the Secondary Classroom. *Principal Leadership*, 64–66.

Fleischer, C., & Andrew-Vaughan, S. (2009). *Writing Outside Your Comfort Zone: Helping Students Navigate Unfamiliar Genres*. Portsmouth, NH: Heinemann.

Fletcher, R. (1992). *What a Writer Needs*. Portsmouth, NH: Heinemann.

Frank, O. H. (1952). *Anne Frank: The Diary of a Young Girl*. New York: Bantam Books.

Fredricksen, J. E., Wilhelm, J. D., & Smith, M. (2012). *So, What's the Story?: Teaching Narrative to Understand Ourselves, Others, and the World*. Portsmouth, NH: Heinemann.

Gallagher, K. (2009). *Readicide: How Schools Are Killing Reading and What You Can Do About It*. Portland, ME: Stenhouse Publishers.

Gallagher, K. (2011). *Write Like This: Teaching Real-World Writing Through Modeling and Mentor Texts*. Portland, ME: Stenhouse Publishers.

Graff, G., Birkenstein, C., & Durst, R. (2011). *"They Say / I Say": The Moves That Matter in Academic Writing with Readings* (2nd ed.). New York: W. W. Norton.

Graves, D. H., & Kittle, P. (2005). *Inside Writing: How to Teach the Details of Craft*. Portsmouth, NH: Heinemann.

Gruwell, E., & The Freedom Writers. (1999). *The Freedom Writers Diary: How a Teacher and 150 Teens Used Writing to Change Themselves and the World Around Them*. New York: Broadway Books.

Hesse, K. (1997). *Out of the Dust*. New York: Scholastic Press.

Hiaasen, C. (2005). *Hoot*. New York: Yearling.

Hicks, T. (2009). *The Digital Writing Workshop*. Portsmouth, NH: Heinemann.

Hillocks, G., Jr. (2011). *Teaching Argument Writing, Grades 6–12: Supporting Claims with Relevant Evidence and Clear Reasoning*. Portsmouth, NH: Heinemann.

Hobbs, R. (2010). *Copyright Clarity: How Fair Use Supports Digital Learning*. Thousand Oaks, CA: Corwin Press.

Hobbs, R. (2011). *Digital and Media Literacy: Connecting Culture and Classroom*. Thousand Oaks, CA: Corwin Press.

International Society for Technology in Education. (2007). The ISTE National Educational Technology Standards (NETS-S) and Performance Indicators for Students. Retrieved from http://iste.org/Content/NavigationMenu/NETS/ForStudents/2007Standards/NETS_for_Students_2007_Standards.pdf

Jetton, T. L., & Shanahan, C. (Eds.). (2012). *Adolescent Literacy in the Academic Disciplines: General Principles and Practical Strategies*. New York: Guilford Press.

Jones, R. (1996). *The Acorn People*. New York: Laurel Leaf.

Kahney, L. (2010, November 18). iPad May Replace Computers and Textbooks In School, Expert Predicts [Apple in Education]. Retrieved from http://www.cultofmac.com/70112/ipad-may-replace-computers-and-textbooks-in-schools-expert-predicts-appli-in-education

Kajder, S. B. (2006). *Bringing the Outside In: Visual Ways to Engage Reluctant Readers*. Portland, ME: Stenhouse Publishers.

Kemp, N. (2010). Texting versus Txtng: Reading and Writing Text Messages, and Links with Other Linguistic Skills. *Writing Systems Research*, 2(1), 53–71. doi:10.1093/wsr/wsq002

Kinney, J. (2011). *Diary of a Wimpy Kid Box of Books*. New York: Amulet Books.

Kittle, P. (2008). *Write Beside Them: Risk, Voice, and Clarity in High School Writing*. Portsmouth, NH: Heinemann.

Kolb, L. (2008). *Toys to Tools: Connecting Student Cell Phones to Education*. Eugene, OR: International Society for Technology in Education.

Lane, B. (2003). *51 Wacky We-Search Reports: Face the Facts With Fun*. Shoreham, VT: Discover Writing Press.

Lattimer, H. (2003). *Thinking through Genre: Units of Study in Reading and Writing Workshops Grades 4–12*. Portland, ME: Stenhouse Publishers.

Lenhart, A. (2009). *Teens and Mobile Phones over the Past Five Years: Pew Internet Looks Back*. Pew Internet and American Life Project. Retrieved from http://pewinternet.org/~/media//Files/Reports/2009/PIP%20Teens%20and%20Mobile%20Phones%20Data%20Memo.pdf

Lenhart, A., Arafeh, S., Smith, A., & Macgill, A. R. (2008). *Writing, Technology and Teens*. Washington D.C.: Pew Internet and American Life Project. Retrieved from http://pewinternet.org/pdfs/PIP_Writing_Report_FINAL3.pdf

London, J. (2012). *The Call of the Wild*. Lexington, KY: Simon & Brown.

Lowry, L. (1989). *Number the Stars*. Boston, MA: Houghton Mifflin.

Lupica, M. (2010). *Million-Dollar Throw*. New York: Puffin Books.

Mathews, J. (2012, October 24). Readers' Cures for Bad Teaching of Writing. *The Washington Post*. Retrieved from http://washingtonpost.com/blogs/class-struggle/post/readers-cures-for-bad-teaching-of-writing/2012/10/24/c1faaeea-1e2f-11e2-9cd5-b55c38388962_blog.html

McBride, L. (2012). *Hold Me Closer, Necromancer*. New York: Square Fish.

Moline, S. (2011). *I See What You Mean: Visual Literacy K–8* (2nd ed.). Portland, ME: Stenhouse Publishers.

MSU News. (2010, September 9). LMK, IDK: Texting is Writing, Researcher Says. MSU Research. Retrieved from http://research.msu.edu/stories/lmk-idk-texting-writing-researcher-says

Murphy Paul, A. (2013, May 3). The New Marshmallow Test: Resisting the Temptations of the Web. Hechinger Report. Retrieved from http://hechinger report.org/content/the-new-marshmallow-test-resisting-the-temptations-of-the-web_11941/

National Council of Teachers of English. (2008). Writing Now: A Policy Research Brief Produced by the National Council of Teachers of English. Retrieved from http://ncte.org/library/NCTEFiles/Resources/PolicyResearch/WrtgResearchBrief.pdf

National Council of Teachers of English. (2011). *Reading and Writing across the Curriculum: A Policy Research Brief*. Urbana, IL: National Council of Teachers of English. Retrieved from http://ncte.org/library/NCTEFiles/Resources/Journals/CC/0203-mar2011/CC0203Policy.pdf

National Council of Teachers of English, & International Reading Association. (1996). NCTE / IRA Standards for the English Language Arts. *NCTE / IRA Standards for the English Language Arts*. Retrieved from http://ncte.org/standards

National Parent Teacher Association. (n.d.). Parents' Guide to Student Success. Retrieved from http://pta.org/parents/content.cfm?ItemNumber=2583

New Media Consortium, Consortium for School Networking, & International Society for Technology in Education. (2012). *Horizon Report: 2012 K–12 Edition*. Retrieved from http://nmc.org/pdf/2012-horizon-report-K12.pdf

Nielsen, L., & Webb, W. (2011). *Teaching Generation Text: Using Cell Phones to Enhance Learning*. San Francisco, CA: Jossey-Bass.

Ohler, J. B. (2010). *Digital Community, Digital Citizen*. Thousand Oaks, CA: Corwin Press.

Palacio, R. J., & Knopf, I. (2012). *Wonder*. New York: Alfred A. Knopf.

Patterson, J., & Park, L. (2012). *I Funny*. New York: Little Brown and Co. Retrieved from http://contentreserve.com/TitleInfo.asp?ID={E92FCE55-7165-48ED-99D9-21FE655D8D02}&Format=410

Paulsen, G. (1987). *Hatchet*. New York: Simon & Schuster.

Paulsen, G. (2011). *The Transall Saga*. New York: Delacorte Press Books for Young Readers.

Plester, B., Wood, C., & Bell, V. (2008). Txt Msg N School Literacy: Does Texting and Knowledge of Text Abbreviations Adversely Affect Children's Literacy Attainment? *Literacy, 42*(3), 137–144. doi:10.1111/j.1741–4369.2008.00489.x

Putz, M. (2006). *A Teacher's Guide to the Multigenre Research Project: Everything You Need to Get Started*. Heinemann. Retrieved from http://amazon.com/dp/0325007853

Ray, K.W. (2010). *In Pictures and In Words: Teaching the Qualities of Good Writing through Illustration Study*. Portsmouth, NH: Heinemann.

Reynolds, G. (2008). *Presentation Zen: Simple Ideas on Presentation Design and Delivery*. Berkeley, CA: New Riders Press.

Reynolds, G. (2010). *The Naked Presenter: Delivering Powerful Presentations With or Without Slides*. Berkeley, CA: New Riders Press.

Robinson, K. (2011). *Out of Our Minds: Learning to be Creative* (2nd ed.). Oxford, UK: Capstone.

Romano, T. (2000). *Blending Genre, Altering Style?: Writing Multigenre Papers*. Portsmouth, NH: Boynton/Cook.

Romano, T. (2007). The Many Ways of Multigenre. In T. Newkirk & R. Kent (Eds.), *Teaching the Neglected "R": Rethinking Writing Instruction in Secondary Classrooms* (pp. 87–102). Portsmouth, NH: Heinemann.

Rothstein, A. (1936). Dust Bowl Farmer Raising Fence to Keep It from Being Buried under Drifting Sand. Cimarron County, Oklahoma. Still image. Retrieved from http://loc.gov/pictures/item/fsa1998018982/PP/

Schmoker, M. (2001, October 24). The "Crayola Curriculum." *Education Week*. Retrieved from http://edweek.org/ew/articles/2001/10/24/08schmoker.h21.html

Sharpe, J. (2010, October 23). The Writing Workshop: A Valuable Tool for Differentiation and Formative Assessment. *Edutopia*. Retrieved from http://edutopia.org/blog/writing-workshop-differentiated-instruction-formative-assessment

Smekens Education Solutions. (2012). Argumentative v. Persuasive Writing. Retrieved from http://smekenseducation.com/argumentative-v-persuasive-writing.html

Smith, M.W., & Wilhelm, J. (2007). *Getting It Right: Fresh Approaches to Teaching Grammar, Usage, and Correctness*. New York: Scholastic Teaching Resources.

Smith, M., Wilhelm, J. D., & Fredricksen, J. E. (2012). *Oh, Yeah?!: Putting Argument to Work both in School and Out*. Portsmouth, NH: Heinemann.

Smith, R. K. (1982). *Jelly Belly*. New York: Yearling.

Swanson, K. (2013). *Teaching the Common Core Speaking & Listening Standards: Strategies & Digital Tools*. Larchmont, NY: Eye on Education.

Stafford, W. (2014). The Osage Orange Tree: A Story by William Stafford. New York: Trinity University Press.

Toulmin, S. E. (2003). *The Uses of Argument*. Cambridge: Cambridge University Press. Retrieved from http://search.ebscohost.com/login.aspx?direct=true& scope=site&db=nlebk&db=nlabk&AN=120780

Treat, L. (2003). *Crime and Puzzlement: 24 Solve-Them-Yourself Picture Mysteries*. Boston, MA: David R Godine.

Troianovski, A. (2013, January 28). The Web-Deprived Study at McDonald's. *Wall Street Journal*. Retrieved from http://online.wsj.com/article/SB100014 24127887324731304578189794161056954.html

Turkle, S. (2011). *Alone Together: Why We Expect More from Technology and Less from Each Other*. New York: Basic Books.

Turner, K. H. (2009). Flipping the Switch: Code-Switching from Text Speak to Standard English. *English Journal*, 98(5), 60–65.

Turner, K. H. (2012). Digitalk as Community. *English Journal*, 101(4), 37–42.

Warschauer, M. (2011). *Learning in the Cloud: How (and Why) to Transform Schools with Digital Media*. New York: Teachers College Press.

Westerfeld, S., & Rosamilia, M. (2011). *Uglies*. New York: Simon Pulse.

Williams, R. (2008). *The Non-Designers Design Book: Design and Typographic Principles for the Visual Novice* (3rd ed.). Berkeley, CA: Peachpit Press.